Timesmart:
How Real People
Really Get Things Done at Home

by

Doug & Gayle Smart

James &
Brookfield
J&B
Publishers

Atlanta, Georgia

Photo: We chose this picture after rejecting 72 posed shots because this is the real us. We are shown here loading up the stuff our college daughter (Amanda) wants to *temporarily* store at home.

TimeSmart:
How Real People Really Get Things Done at Home

For more information, contact:
James & Brookfield Publishers
P.O. Box 768024
Roswell, GA 30076
(770) 587-9784

Library of Congress Catalog Number: 97-73843

ISBN: 0-9658893-3-5

10 9 8 7 6 5 4 3 2 1

Dedicated to Gram, Doris Ergas

My Grandmother is the *Queen of Time Management.*
I remember Saturday afternoons as a little girl waiting for
Gram to arrive. She worked Saturday mornings in New
York City and took the train to Long Island in the
afternoon to spend the weekend with us. No sooner did
Gram get in the house than she would start unpacking her
shopping bag filled with goodies — like spaghetti and
meatballs with sauce already cooked (our favorite)! One
of Gram's organizational secrets — pack on Friday nights
(hat, gloves, money, train schedule, treats for my sister
and me, shopping bag).

Today, at 94 years young, Gram lives in her own
apartment, manages her own finances, and mails birthday
cards filled with love.

You are the greatest, Gram!
We love you.

Table of Contents

Getting Started: Energized & Organized in the A.M.
Start the Morning the Night Before ● Face Forward ● Start by Reading ● First One in Gets a Hot Shower ● Some Things You Can Do Ahead of Time ● Here's One Way to Not be Late ● Prepare for a Good Morning ● The Maun Method ● Who's on First? ● Drive Time is Your Time ● Ready to Wear ● Planning Ahead Can be Easy ● Avoiding the Bathroom Bottleneck ● It Just Takes a Solid 30 Minutes ● Mess with the Clock ● Getting Dressed is a Snap ● Include the Car in Your Daily Preparation

Quick & Easy Organizational Systems for Time Management that's a Snap
Begin with a Plan for the Day ● Start with a Large Calendar Next to the Phone ● Organizing Notes ● Make Notes for the Weekend ● A Notebook Works, Too ● Prioritize the To Do List ● Scheduling Helps Share the Duties ● Viva the Junk Drawer! ● A System, Simple & Straight-forward ● Kids' Daily Responsibilities ● Keep Up with Details with This System ● Calendar System ● Refrigerator Scheduling ● Managing Personal Affairs ● Put a Daily Planner to Work for You ● Be a Role Model

INTRODUCTION

TimeSmart adj: *describes a person who knows how to get the right things done at the right time. Implies a person of above average productivity and noteworthy achievement; one who is clever, well respected for accomplishments and frequently recognized as a leader;* **-er** : *a better way.*

To the TimeSmart people quoted in this book, thank you for sharing your wisdom with us. As Doug traveled and met you, I was back home with our son, Jimmy, keeping the Smart household TimeSmart.

The Bradys Moved. Real People Live Here Now

We are *real people*, too. You might be wondering, are *we* totally organized and always on time? To which we reply, *get real!* Like you, we are on a hyper-speed learning journey through life. There is always a better way and we are willing to try. We know more this year than last (*a lot more* after reading the hundreds of responses you flooded us with for both this book and its companion, *TimeSmart: How Real People Really Get Things Done at <u>Work</u>*). And we expect to be even better educated next year.

Let me give you an idea of what it's like in our house. Many a Sunday afternoon, no matter how well organized we think we are, we have a 45 minute whirlwind of packing activity just before Doug goes off to the airport. Just two weeks ago, Doug arrived in Pittsburgh without his suit pants! They were still at home. How could this minor catastrophe have happened? We both had picked up the pants and moved them around the room to get them out of the way as Doug packed. We thought we were being efficient. But like I said, there is always a better way.

How This Book Came About

In the classic teacher/student relationship, who always learns more? The teacher, of course. As a professional speaker and consultant, my husband, Doug Smart, is always in front of people. And he always ends the day knowing more than when he started. So, as he tells it, he got smart and started writing down their ideas. After a while he got smarter and started asking them to write down their own valuable how tos and give them to him so the knowledge can be shared with others who might be stuck trying to re-invent the wheel. This book is loaded with tips and suggestions about how to set home goals, get organized, get started, and gain the cooperation of the people around you. Home, the way we see it, should be a very low stress, *safe harbor* place that refreshes and rein-vigorates us so we can sail back into the sea of work.

We have tried many of these ideas (but not all) in our home and they work. The process is fun and the insight gained is keen. The best part — you and I can avoid dis-appointments and wasted time and money by benefiting from the field-tested wisdom of so many people.

All of the ideas in this book work for the people who wrote them. Some might seem to contradict others. But that's okay. If we homogenized the thoughts and only included the ones we agreed with you wouldn't get the benefit of a richly diverse mixture of solutions. And besides, you and I know that the ideas we are most likely to personally adopt are the ones that fit our personalities, style, and help us to quickly become the kind of people we aspire to be. When you find two opposite ways of traveling to the same destination, resist the temptation to think they cancel out each other; simply choose the one that is a more comfortable route for you.

We did grammar polishing here and there. Some awkward sentences begged to be paraphrased, so we accommodated. The intent was to make the suggestions easier to read. But basically this book is real people telling it like it is in their own words. Enjoy, keep an open mind, be willing to experiment with new twists on old challenges, and when you finish — write down a couple of TimeSmart ideas of your own and send them to us so that your hard learned wisdom can help make life better for others!

A Caution

By reading a book you and I will not suddenly start getting *everything* done. Why? No one gets it all done. No matter how much we accomplish there is always more to do. Okay, but if we can't get it all done, can we at least focus on getting the right things done at the right time? Yes. TimeSmart is *getting the right things done at the right time.*

Chapter I
Getting Started:
Energized & Organized
in the A.M.

Dost thou love life?
Then do not squander time,
for that is the stuff life is made of.
BENJAMIN FRANKLIN

When I look into the future,
it's so bright it burns my eyes.
OPRAH WINFREY

Start the Morning the Night Before

Renee Gallart of Conifer, CO is a trainer by profession.
Trainers know the best way to get a message across is to
just tell it like it is. Renee says, "things get done when I'm
rested. I only rest when I clear my brain of any and all
things I think I need to do." To clear her mind before
retiring for the evening, she makes "a list, just before

bedtime, of all the things I want to achieve [the next day.] I catch my ZZZ's and when I awake, I feel refreshed, and ready to prioritize."

Face Forward

We think Mitch Timberlake of Orange Park, FL is onto something here. "Upon returning home," Mitch advises, "back the car into the garage. This allows you to start the day by driving out of the garage going forward, not starting off in reverse."

Start by Reading

The Center for Fiber-Optic Testing is where Brian Harpster of Painted Post, NY works. His advice for starting the morning on a positive note: "the first thirty minutes of each day are best spent clearing your mind before you get to work." Good advice. How do you do it? For me (Doug), I include reading for 10 minutes every morning — first thing out of bed. I grab something that is inspirational, motivational, or how to. It's like brain groceries. Many of us are conscientious about what we eat, but maybe we don't put enough attention on what we feed our heads. I consider reading for 10 minutes every morning a *brain vitamin*. And as they used to say on TV ads, "it really really works!" Denis Waitley, a counselor to Olympic level athletes, notes in *The Psychology of Winning*, "we become what we think about." For example, people who want to become really good at growing vegetables absorb their gardening catalogs and books; if you want an exceptionally beautiful home, you love to read the decorating magazines; if your desire is to be the top electrician in your city, you take great pleasure in learning how the champions of your industry overcame the lions, tigers, and bears of adversity. Reading for ten minutes first thing in the morning is a fun, relaxing/stimulating way to frame your day in a positive, successful light.

Rachel Kelly, a physical therapist in Versailles, KY has long known the power of a morning read. "Most mornings while I eat breakfast," says Rachel, I spend 10-15 minutes reading, whether it be a magazine for pleasure, a journal article for work, or a chapter in a book. I used to say I never had time to read for pleasure but now I find that I can finish an entire book in a few weeks!" Cruising at 10 to 15 pages a morning, it does not take long to finish a 200 page book.

First One in Gets a Hot Shower

Do several people share a bathroom in your home? Here is how our college daughter, Amanda Smart, meets the challenge of communal life. "I live in a dorm with 16 girls on my floor and a bathroom with only one working shower," says Amanda. "Everyone has to get ready for 8 a.m. class. I get up at 6:15 and run to take a shower (I have to be early to get a hot shower. It's an old building.) and there is no line at that time."

Some Things You Can Do Ahead of Time

Our high school senior, Jimmy Smart, has to be out the
front door every morning at 6:15. He faces a challenge
a lot of us know too well — he is a night person with an
early wake-up call. Wide-awake in the late evening, occasionally he will stay up to catch the end of a baseball or
basketball game on TV. How does he maximize the barest
minimum of morning time? "Shave and pick out your
clothes the night before, know where your shoes are,
and once a week catch an afternoon nap," are Jimmy's
recommendations.

Here's One Way to Not be Late

"All the clocks in my home are set ahead twenty minutes," according to Betsy Gabbard of Gainesville, FL.
"This gets the kids to school on time and me to work
early to get focused" on attacking the day's challenges
with a fresh start.

Prepare for a Good Morning

Lauren Howell lives in East Peoria, IL and manages a
botanical garden. To get her family rolling in the morning,
Lauren says, "I pack the diaper bag, school backpack,
lunches and my briefcase before I go to bed at night. In
the morning I get myself ready before I get the kids up
(of course sometimes they have their own agendas!) and
get them ready. This keeps the conflicts to a minimum
and saves time." And it makes for a happier and more
refreshing start to the day.

The Maun Method

A pre-school teacher, Teri Maun of Tulsa, OK, has a delightful way of teaching her own little ones how to be ready in the morning in a relaxed, unrushed way (which will probably help them as adults to avoid ulcers and nervous breakdowns!). Teri tells us, "friends call this the *Maun Method*. Fifteen minutes before bed, as a family, here is what we do:

1. Each child's uniform is hung on the closet door (including ribbons, socks, underwear, and shoes). Rule: You may not change your mind. [As a role model,] I even set my clothes out.
2. Backpacks are filled and put by the front door. Some friends [who use this method, too,] even put them in the car.
3. Lunches and snacks are made and put in the refrigerator.
4. The table is set with bowls and cereal for break-fast. Then a short list of anything special needed for school — with those items — is set on the table by the bowls. NOTE: you may not come down to breakfast until completely dressed. The reasoning: it really only takes fifteen minutes at night [to prepare for the morn-ing] compared to changing minds and endless searching in the morning.
5. Then it's off to school (me, too). The girls know [I play by the rules, too and] I can not go back for forgotten items either.

The girls like this system, are not rushed, and often have time to themselves before school."

Who's on First?

Pam Heissenbrittel, a physical therapist in Lexington, KY has the fast thinking organizational ability of an air traffic controller. Here is Pam's story of how she gets five people up, showered, dressed, teeth brushed, beds made, fed, and off to conquer the world in only 50 minutes. She writes, "I have three boys (14,13,7) and a husband, so my mornings are rather hectic. In the mornings we set priorities and stay on schedule in order to get all of the things done before we leave the house at 7:20. Most of the organization takes place the night before to reduce the morning stress for everyone. Lunches are made, backpacks ready, and clothes chosen for the day. At 6:30 I wake up son #1. I go turn on the shower, he makes his bed and I set a timer for four minutes. The four minute timer is our salvation. On the way back to my room, I wake son #2 and then get on with my routine. When the timer goes off son #1 finishes his shower while son #2 makes his bed and wakes son #3. Then #2 goes to the shower and the timer is set by #1 for four minutes, then he goes on with his morning. Son #3 gets up when he hears the alarm (he doesn't shower) but that's when #2 gets out! Miraculously, everyone is finished and downstairs within twenty minutes (and rather painlessly I might add.) All beds are made, breakfast eaten, teeth brushed, and everyone ready in fifty minutes. It sounds complicated but it's not. The prearranged plan decreases stress and conflicts and increases efficiency. We're all out the door on time because working together we accomplish a great deal."

Drive Time is Your Time

Does morning rush hour traffic have you sometimes feeling edgy and stressed before you even get a chance to dig into the real challenges of the day? Try doing what Janice Purtell of Milwaukee, WI does. "I seldom listen to the radio during my 45 minute drive in to work," Janice says. "This is the perfect time to organize and prioritize my professional and personal responsibilities." It works in reverse, too. "On the drive home I can sort through the day, unwind, and arrive home able to leave work behind."

Ready to Wear

Some mornings *what to wear?* is a mind numbing decision. Jo Hopkins of Champaign, IL has a nifty solution. "With [daily planner] book in hand, [so you will see what meetings and other events you are dressing for,] choose your wardrobe for each day — complete from earrings to shoes. Clip the hangers together with clothes pins and label each set for the day of week. In the morning, grab appropriate set — no thinking involved." And go!

Planning Ahead Can be Easy

Fanny Marie Rochester of Palm Bay, FL recommends, "prepare yourself for the next day before you go to bed." Her can't-be-beat method:

1. Get clothing together.
2. Prepare shoes, polish or check colors.

3. Check stockings.

4. Prepare envelope for church if going to church.

5. Keep keys in purse or in one place.

Avoiding the Bathroom Bottleneck

"To manage being out the door in the morning for school and work, we had to make bathroom time," says Rebecca Dixon of Lafayette, IN. Fast showers are fine sometimes, but having time to yourself to get bathed and dressed is pure luxury. How to accommodate three people? "My daughter chose to take her bath or shower in the evening , therefore she only gets 10-15 minutes in the morning. I get up at 4:45 and am out of the bathroom by 5:30. Larry takes 6:15 to 7:00. This way we're all out the door on time for buses and work. My daughter knows if she's not ready for school, she will be on the bus in her night clothes, so she gets going!"

It Just Takes a Solid 30 Minutes

Susanne McCalla is a materials logistics manager in Ocala, FL and brings her expertise to organizing the work flow in her home. "Being a full time manager and mother of two, ages 4 and 3," Susanne informs us, "I find it very important to spend as much time with my kids and husband as possible. I've found that if I get up 30 minutes earlier than really needed in the mornings I can accomplish many household tasks. For example, unload the dishwasher, put on a load of wash, fold some clothes, pick up around the house and most important, load the crockpot up so dinner's ready when we get home. It's amazing what 30 minutes of quality time will get you. Nights are not as crazy as they were at one time and I can relax!" Of course, Susanne is right. In the business world, time management experts cannot resist pointing out that 30 minutes better utilized each work day is the same as two and a half high productivity hours a week, which is the same as 125 top achievement hours per year, which is the same as three solid weeks of peak performance annually!

Mess with the Clock

"I used to have a problem with having enough time to get ready for work," confesses Rhonda Guinn of Bluff City, TN, "until I started setting my alarm clock ahead 5 minutes." Now she finds that the extra 5 minutes acts as a buffer to help transition from sleep to the routine of getting up. "I know it sounds silly, but it really works for me," she adds.

"My husband gets up very early in the morning to go to work," says Wendy Jenkins of Hilliard, OH. "He is a chronic *snooze button* fiend. There are many mornings when he gets up just in the nick of time to make it to work on time. When I secretly set the time ahead 10 to 15 minutes without his knowledge, he gets a couple of extra *snoozes.*" On the back of her note, Wendy added a P.S.: "He catches on to me and resets the clock. I set it ahead again and he'll reset it again. One morning he thought I had set it ahead so he slept in. He was late for work!"

Getting Dressed is a Snap

"Plan your work outfit the night before," recommends
Annette Higgins of St. Louis, MO. "Organize shoes, belts,
and accessories. Iron if needed and have everything ready.
This avoids last minute searching and frustration when
you might be running late for work."

Include the Car in Your Daily Preparation

"With children it is difficult to get out of the house on
time in the morning," observes Terri Valentine of
Fallbrook, CA. "Therefore, you should load everything in
the car the night before."

Being TimeSmart
Turn Your Thoughts to Tools

I. Identify TimeSmart ideas of your own that are inspired by this chapter.

II. Solution seeking
   1. Identify a productivity sapping challenge you occasionally face.

   2. If you could change it from challenge to ideal, what would ideal be like?

   3. Put check marks next to 3 ideas in this chapter that can help you successfully overcome the challenge.

   4. Identify action steps to change the situation for the better and indicate when you will start each one.

Chapter II
Quick & Easy Organizational Systems that Make Time Management a Snap

You have removed most of the roadblocks to success
when you have learned the difference
between movement and direction.
JOE GRIFFITH

Begin with a Plan for the Day

Days have not stopped being 24 hours long. However, with so many things to accomplish, like getting the family started in the morning, packing lunches, maneuvering through traffic, running errands on lunch break, shuffling kids, pets, and maybe even parents to check-ups and appointments, and then preparing a delightful meal so the family can enjoy quality time, it feels like the days have shrunk faster than a sponge in the sun! Mindy Rooney, a processing analyst with an insurance company in Charlotte, NC, sets up her day in a way that helps maximize her time. "Ten years ago I took a time management course. The best thing that came out of that class for me was the A B C—1 2 3 method of prioritizing tasks. The critical ones ([which are] probably the tasks you least want to face) received an A. All 'A's' were grouped for the day then assigned a number in the order in which they were to be accomplished." B items were important but not critical. And C items are good stuff but if they never got done, life as we know it would still go on. That is a fast and effective method for organizing your day. Mindy adds, "it may seem simple but it works for me."

Start with a Large Calendar Next to the Phone

"Family life can be so hectic with three children, both parents working full time and a husband trying to build his own business part time. I was finding myself forgetting appointments and due dates," says Joyce Bolton of Manassas, VA, a manager in federal government. The solution? "I bought a large desktop size calendar (one month displayed at a time) and put it on the counter in the kitchen by the phone where I keep all the mail. As appointments are made, I jot them (in pencil) on the calendar; as I get appointments in the mail or from my kids' paperwork, I jot them down. It has kept my life easier and less stressful. I also keep a 3 x 5 card next to the calendar and write down things as they come up for my to do list for Saturday errands."

Organizing Notes

Manufacturing engineer Larry Stokwski recommends keeping track of details like this: "take Post-it Notes and as ideas come, put them on a calendar. Then put the Post-it's in order for a things to do list [for that day]"

Make Notes for the Weekend

Mary Pinkerton of Rogers, AR, tells us how she maximizes her *off day* accomplishments: "I keep 3 x 5 note cards at my desk in the kitchen. During the week when I'm busy and think of things I need to do on my day off, I jot them down. Then on my day off I gather them up and prioritize them. A lot of times I find that I get more done. And by writing them down I don't worry about them all week."

A Notebook Works, Too

Collecting thoughts on 3 x 5 cards is a TimeSmart idea for staying on top of important items that are to be done later. But what about daily planning? Joe Kirsch of Tulsa, OK, says, "for time management, I use a small spiral notebook. I date each day and page, using two pages if needed." He then jots down what he would like to get accomplished that day. An extra benefit of this simple method, the notebooks become permanent logs of his activities and can be useful resources for looking up "old" information.

Prioritize the To Do List

"I use a to do list," reports Ella Cheatham of Oklahoma City, "usually prioritized 1 to 3. I leave room for disruptions. At home I list all chores and errands to do and I check them off as I accomplish them. I try not to overload my plate; I work on having a well balanced life."

Scheduling Helps Share the Duties

When a job is bigger than one person can handle, try scheduling the time so that others can work with you. "When my mother was sick with cancer she needed full time attention. Dad couldn't do it all himself," Jo Ann Bateman of Maud, OK writes. "All eight of us kids had families and jobs. So what we did was, have dad take care of her during the day (he was retired) and then one of us kids would come in around 7:00 p.m. to take care of her. Later one of the other kids came in and relieved that one at 2:00 a.m. That way no one missed work or family time and we got to take care of our mother [through the night] like she did for us years ago."

Viva the Junk Drawer!

Bob Griffin is an instructional systems specialist with the U.S. Army. Bob believes "in your home you need a place for everything and everything in it's place." That said, he offers this very logical, civilized, TimeSmart advice for staying organized and un-stressed: "you must have a junk drawer to put things in. That way you don't waste time

Kids' Daily Responsibilities

and effort trying to figure out where to put every little thing you get or own."

A System, Simple & Straight-forward

Kevin Collins, a data base administrator in Peoria, IL, believes in simplifying life at home. His family recipe is:

> *Dinner* at 5:30
> *Homework* at 6:30
> *Playtime* at 7:30
> *Bedtime* at 8:30

Kids' Daily Responsibilities

Dr. Dana Mollenkopf, an elementary school principal in Richmond, IN, says, "my wife and I have always felt it to be important for our children to have daily responsibilities. With their input, a list of jobs was developed. Each job was put on a separate Post-it Note. We placed a school picture of each of them on the side of the refrigerator. The notes were put in a column between them. Each day two or three chores were moved under their pictures. Once completed, the note was returned to the column for future use."

Keep Up with Details with This System

Here are neat ideas that can save hours of frustration in hunting down important minutia. This comes from Kim

Wroblewski of New Haven, IN, who works for the U.S. Postal Service. "Keep a list of those things that you buy or need a record of when you are away from the house. Tuck it into your purse or portfolio. [Jot down things like:]

- The family's Social Security numbers
- Type of sweeper bag you use
- Furnace filter size
- Directions to the farm you buy straw at yearly
- Your kid's car make, model, and license plate numbers — in case you want to call the state police.

Kim, who sounds like she is wonderful at keeping track of details, also recommends, "keep a Rolodex card file [of important people in your life and next to the] phone numbers and names, list everything possible on the card about that person — things like: kids names, anniversary dates, the school the kids attend, and where they work. For instance, if you are interacting with people through committees on a regular basis, it helps to personalize your conversation by asking about the kids, the job, and their interests. Directions to their house are also helpful."

Calendar System

Marcia deKramer is a school counselor in Alexandria, VA and she has a system for keeping important day to day information in one spot. "Using a small calendar (one from a bank or business), I record various events of the day in my own shorthand," says Marcia. "It's the calendar we keep by the phone, so after a year it's chock full of information. I save these calendars (they don't take up much space) and they become a point of reference. [They have] real important information that I might have to search for in files otherwise. I learned this technique from my mother-in-law."

Refrigerator Scheduling

"I have a routine to get things done," Michelle Brown of Manito, IL shares with us. However, the world does not always adhere to our schedule. How to stay up with the adjustments? "I keep a list on our refrigerator," says Michelle, "of the things that do not fall within the routine of everyday. It works well — from finding clothes for the next day to getting my son in a routine."

Sandy Tucker, a biologist in Kearneysville, WI, successfully uses the refrigerator system, too, to keep her focused on getting stuff done. "I keep a to do list on the refrigerator, not a long list, just the biggest things," she reports. "The visual reminder keeps me from forgetting what I should do."

"As a single mom," says Pauline Lamia, RN of Rancho Mirage, CA., "time is very important and I try to organize my time carefully. I have a very large calendar that takes up the side of my fridge. It is a one year calendar on a single sheet. All medical, dental, car care, child activities, and others appointments are placed here. Each day as I leave for work, I look at it."

Managing Personal Affairs

Administrative assistant, Angie Huffman of Abingdon, VA, knows how to get the right things done at the right time. "Managing priorities at work is easy when compared to managing my personal affairs," she says. "My day timer is used for both business and personal, I keep it with me at all times. I make notes of appointments for me and all family members. In the morning while we are all getting ready for work and school, I ask each family member (usually as we pass in the hall or bathroom) if they have anything special happening that day. A grocery list is kept on the refrigerator and errands are listed in my daily planner until there are several. I run each errand when I am in that area or in the order they appear, on the way to and from work. When possible I keep the majority of *have to do's* in the middle of the work week and save the *want to do's* for the weekend. I spend a lot of time in the car (taking kids to sporting events, etc.) and I keep a book in the car for relaxation. I also keep my checkbook ledger and upcoming bills that need to be paid in my daily planner. While waiting on the kids I can read, balance my checkbook, or write checks for bills."

Put a Daily Planner to Work for You

In order to keep up with my schedule, my children's schedules, and Scout activities, I use a daily planner. I use a different highlighter color for each child and for myself, to mark meetings and work deadlines. As activities come up I mark them on my monthly calendar. On Sunday nights I transfer the activities to the weekly calendar. This includes reports and projects that the children have due at school and Scouts."

Be a Role Model

Geraldine Hubbard of Monterey, CA writes, "I believe preparation is important, especially when dealing with my family. I have a 15 year old and a 5 year old. I always plan almost a week in advance for *everything* including meals, recreation, and other activities. I'm training my children to think and plan ahead so time won't run away, This helps them appreciate time."

Being TimeSmart
Turn Your Thoughts to Tools

I. Identify TimeSmart ideas of your own that are inspired by this chapter.

II. Solution seeking
   1. Identify a productivity sapping challenge you occasionally face.

   2. If you could change it from challenge to ideal, what would ideal be like?

   3. Put check marks next to 3 ideas in this chapter that can help you successfully overcome the challenge.

   4. Identify action steps to change the situation for the better and indicate when you will start each one.

Chapter III
Handling Paper:
Conquer Clutter &
Get the Bills Paid on Time!

Yesterday is a canceled check;
tomorrow is a promissory note;
today is the only cash you have so spend it wisely.
KAY LYONS

Touch it Once

When it comes to dealing with the mail, Susan L. Bevill, a computer operator in Jacksonville, FL, offers this advice, "touch it once, especially junk mail. Read, file it or trash it. Don't put it aside only to pick it up again, unless you are going to use it as a reminder." In handling bills, some like to pay them immediately and others file them for the appropriate paying day. The point is, try not to let them sit in a stress-causing stack on the kitchen counter until the day of reckoning.

Shirley Jean Holman of Nashville, TN agrees. "Open mail," she says, "over a trash can. Don't even take junk mail inside."

Organizing Bills & Payments

Brandan Laura of Tarzana, CA offers a sensible method for dealing with bill handling. "As each bill comes in," suggests Brandan, "open it, write the amount due and the date due on the outside of the envelope, and put the bill back in the envelope. Keep all bills in one stack with the soonest due on top. Keep stack in a visible place on desk at home. Three days prior to due date, pay bill, writing the amount paid and the date on the portion you keep. Put together a notebook (a one and a half inch three ring binder is ideal) and label it as current year's bills. Use dividers and label each as a different category (examples: bank statements, phone, utilities, taxes, credit cards)." File the paid bills and you have a permanent record that is easy for quick filing and easy to use for locating old transactions. For tax keeping, this organization system sounds ideal. When figuring your taxes you have all you need in some categories already grouped together — beats hunting them up. And if you ever get audited, the last thing you want to put your energy into is scrambling to find old receipts that might otherwise be scattered through the files.

Storing Financial Records

"At home I do not file or throw away my paid bills, " reports Fred Collie a police lieutenant living in Arlington, TX. "I put them in a paper box and I can refer to them later if needed. At the end of the year, I can tape the box up and store it or dispose of it. This saves filing time and filing space and ensures I have a record of the bills if needed."

Short Stint Method

"Financial paperwork bores me, scares me and is something I've always put off," Dorinda Reed of Excelsior, MN shares with us. "When my first husband, who had always handled these matters, passed away, I needed to do a lot of financial paperwork. I learned to do this work responsibly and competently by using this method: I lay out the necessary papers on my desk, sit down and audibly remind myself of three things:

> 1. I'm grateful I have the time to do this work (as much time as it takes)
> 2. I'm grateful I have the intelligence to figure this out.
> 3. I'm grateful I have the money to pay these bills, taxes, whatever.

"Then I decide on a time limit for this session of work. I usually decide to sit there and work for one hour, after which I can get up and go do something more relaxing or interesting. With that promise to myself I know I can work at least that long. Almost always that hour of work gets me past my own resistance and I forget the clock and end up working for two or three hours. I have used the same method (I call it my *stint method*) to accomplish other kinds of work I might find myself resisting."

Colorful Filing System that Works

"Use different colored folders for different projects," is Kathy Kuhl DiSalvo's advice. "At home, keep a file cabinet with folders for each topic. For magazines or catalogues tear out the article and cover, staple them and file them if you don't have time to read or order from them now. Keep catalogs in alphabetical order; on a daily basis, when you get a new catalog, throw out the previous issue. Anything unused for two years, get rid of. Label and date everything."

3 Cool Filing Systems to Simplify Home Life

Beth Sabez of Milwaukee, WI sounds to us like an organizational expert. Beth offers these TimeSmart ideas:

"1. I utilize a *tickler file*. It's simply an expandable file folder that has 31 pockets (one for each day of the month). I use it to collect notes, reminders, and to do's for that particular day." Be sure to check it everyday and important details will not fall through the cracks.

2. I have a *bill box*. I use a plastic box with dividers labeled 1-31. Whenever I receive a bill I file it approximately one week before it is due. I look in this box daily or jot [down references to it] in red on the calendar.

3. I also have a *would like to do jar*. I put notes in the jar of what I would like to do: scrub floors, wash windows, or really clean the bathroom. I pull one note out on Monday and I get the job done by next Monday. I feel good because I accomplished a wish."

Touch it Once

Hard Copy Tickler File

"The hard copy tickler file has been the most important step
I've made lately to improve my self-esteem!" says Teresa
Lee, a high school teacher in Doniphan, MO. "I couldn't get
my bills paid on time, make reservations, find confirmation
slips... I felt like an imbecile! Years ago I worked several
months as a payroll clerk for a brake lever factory. Using
such a file was part of my job. It took me about 15 years to
realize I could use that idea in my own life. Duh! I carry it
with me always. It's in a plastic file case, the skinny one, as
I open my mail the junk is trashed and the bills are filed. It
goes with me on trips, to school, everywhere. Many times
I'm caught waiting somewhere, so I open my mail, and deal
with it immediately. I'm human again and my credit rating
has improved."

A choir director in Jackson, MS, Jeanette Anderson
Englehart remembers, "my parents always used a tickler
file with dividers in the box for 1-15 and 16-31, which
helped them pay bills, keep information together for
dentist and doctor visits, and in general maintain some sort
of organized scheduling in a family with four busy kids."

Tickler File Makes Finding Paperwork a Snap

"The single most useful time management strategy I have
ever used at home is my *tickler file*," says Holladay
Thompson of Champaign, IL. I have the large expandable
kind with 31 day files and 12 month files. Because of this
system, I eliminated all other *current* files. Here's how it
works: I designate certain days for certain tasks, for example on the first and fifteenth pay bills; on the fifth do bank

reconciliation; on the twentieth I handle paperwork for the association I'm an officer in.

"With this file system, all mail now goes in the appropriate date or in the garbage. For instance, a sale flyer or concert ticket goes in the date of the event. Any information I'm not sure about goes in the general file for the next month. Just be sure to review tomorrow's file today and plan tomorrow's to do's. On the last day of the each month, when I move items from the general monthly file to the day files, I review them and then act on, file, or toss."

Holladay also adds this, "remember when you move greeting cards from month to day, move them to mail date, not actual date."

Everything in One Place

"My husband, a former Marine, had to move sometimes at a moment's notice," says Cheryl DeNoi, a teacher in Covina, CA. "He kept all of his financial and personal records along with account numbers, birthdays, and other important data in one heavy-duty manila folder with little collapsible arms inside (to hold hole-punched papers). He has been using this method for 22 years and has never been without it."

Being TimeSmart
Turn Your Thoughts to Tools

I. Identify TimeSmart ideas of your own that are inspired by this chapter.

II. Solution seeking
   1. Identify a productivity sapping challenge you occasionally face.

   2. If you could change it from challenge to ideal, what would ideal be like?

   3. Put check marks next to 3 ideas in this chapter that can help you successfully overcome the challenge.

   4. Identify action steps to change the situation for the better and indicate when you will start each one.

Chapter IV
Streamlining Home Projects for Increased Leisure Time

*Nothing will ever be attempted
if all possible objections must first be overcome.*
SAMUEL JOHNSON

Simple Formula for Home Project Success

Benny Shoults of Powell, OH, tells us he tackles large home projects best by following an uncomplicated three stage process. He says:

"1. I visualize the completed project.

2. I break it down into small doable pieces that inspire me. This makes me feel good about getting things done.

3. The inspiration helps me complete the smaller projects necessary to complete the whole project.

Sooner Is Better Than Later

To keep little problems from becoming major catastrophes, Lewis Jefferies of Charlotte, NC recommends, "as soon as a visual inspection shows needed repair work in the near future, place a note in a to do basket." On your next trip to the local building supply store the needed "parts can be bought in advance. Repair work can be done *before* an emergency occurs. Unlike an emergency repair, this timely repair will save" both time and money.

The Night Before is Great Time to Make a List

"When I have a lot of tasks to do at home (for example: getting ready for entertaining guests), before going to bed I make a list of all the things I want to accomplish the next day. In the morning I start one task at a time and as I complete it, I cross it off my list. It gives me a great sense of accomplishment as I cross more and more off the list, and it motivates me to stay focused so that I finish everything." This recommendation comes from Karen Obermark of Washington, MO.

Tickler File Helps Schedule Routine Projects

Greg Benedict of Clear Lake, IA, is also a believer in using a tickler file system. He uses his to stay up to date on household projects. Greg informs us, "I use a tickler file to plan work around the house. Each month I list the duties to be done that month so I can schedule time for the tasks. Example: October: rake leaves, store motorcycles for winter, put on storm windows. November: check snowblower for operation. December: put up Christmas tree and decorations. January: take down and store decorations, get oil changed on truck. February: take car for 30,000 mile checkup. This works well if you use a paper organizer or a computer based organizer. It is the best way I've found to make sure I get everything done in a timely manner."

Try Theme Nights

For getting lots of little things accomplished each week, try an idea of Sue Kim's who lives in Los Angeles, CA. "We have *themes* for each day/night of the week. For example, Monday is a resting night, Tuesday is left open, Wednesday is for cleaning." Set the rest up any way you like, such as Thursday is for shopping, Friday is for Date Night (getting dressed up and taking the young children out for dinner and a movie), Saturday could be for yard work, and so on. "Map out the week on Sunday night. But," adds Sue, "You must be flexible and be sure to keep in mind any after-hours meetings or community work you might be involved in."

Break The Task into Manageable Pieces

Lisa Maseng of Columbia, SC says, "I used to feel overwhelmed watering the three areas of my lawn: front, side and back. Now I water my lawn in three stages.

1. Front yard when I get up in the morning before work
2. Side yard when I get home from work
3. Back yard after dinner until I go to bed

"To fertilize your lawn, save money and cool down all at the same time, plan to spread fertilizer during a light rain storm (without any lightning of course!) This way you don't incur a high water bill since there is a natural source and you beat the heat in a cool rain."

Checklists Simplify Life

Sometimes when we change our routine, for example: when preparing for a party at home or leaving for a weekend mini-vacation, important but unfamiliar things get overlooked (like, forgot to buy ice!) and time, energy, and frustration get heaped on something that never should have been a major issue. James T. Hines of Palmetto, GA shares with us a TimeSmart idea that you can count on to save you grief. "Make a special list of things to do or to be accomplished. We do a lot of weekend camping and each time would always forget some item we needed. We make a master check list for this event and pull it out before we go and check off tasks as they are completed. Some are done days before and some right up until it's time to leave. We seldom ever miss anything on our trips now."

Plug In Kid Power

"When undertaking a family project, let the children have as much authority as possible depending on their ages," John Strapp, an industrial engineer with Siemens in Urbana, OH, reminds us.

Reward Yourself

Reward Yourself

"I've always been a list person," confesses Christine Albert
of Salt Lake City, UT, "but I have to also include rewards on
mine! I hate housework so I usually put off cleaning projects
(like scrubbing the bathroom) until the eleventh hour. What
really helps me a lot is, I make a list of all the stuff I have to
get accomplished that day. I put a star by my least favorite.
When I complete that task, I reward myself — take a walk
around the block, get an ice cream sandwich from the freezer,
or something like that. I find that knowing there is a reward
at the end gives me a shot of energy to get the job done and
motivates me to keep going."

Go Ahead, Read the Instructions First

Research done by the duPont Corporation discovered that
time invested in planning is returned 4 to 1. They found
that 15 minutes of planning something will probably
shorten the time it takes to do the entire project by an
hour. But do adults read instructions anymore? We do.
And Linda Graham of Jacksonville, FL does, too. "I save
time by reading things first before doing!" she says. "This
saves a tremendous amount of time at work and in the
kitchen!" Sure does.

And all of this reminds us of our good friend, Jeanne
Chambers, who recently had this outgoing message on her
answering machine, "if at first you don't succeed, look in
the trash can for the instructions! We can't come to the
phone right now because we are busy searching the trash
cans, so leave your message…"

Inch by Inch It's a Cinch

"I used to not be able to get much done around the house and yard until I learned to *plan* major projects such as painting inside rooms or cleaning the outside of the house," says Michael Elkins of Lexington, SC. Some of these projects "require several small projects, such as cleaning, dusting, or minor landscaping, in order to prepare for the major one!" In pursuing the main objective, Michael finds he "accomplishes a lot in its preparation."

Start Early, Finish Early

Shirley Cunningham has a philosophy of accomplishment. "At home," she says, "I start my work early in the morning to make sure I am done by noon. If there is something that needs to be pre-cleaned I do it at night."

Painting Tip

Marsha Williams of Big Stone Gap, VA offers this advice for simplifying handling of painting tools. "When I painted," says Marsha, "I had a problem with cleaning paint rollers and brushes if I did not finish the job that day. Now I put them in plastic bags, seal, and refrigerate. They stay fresh and wet. There is no drying if kept three days or less."

Remodeling? Don't Live In

Nancy Frazier, a critical care nurse in Kingsport, TN, is living in her home while it is being remodeled. The job was supposed to take three months ("You'll have it by Christmas.") and the unfinished project is about to celebrate its first anniversary. Nancy has a great sense of humor but she is so distraught over the disruption in their lives she told Doug she wants to go on *Oprah* to tell the world: "Remodeling? DON'T LIVE IN THE HOUSE WHILE IT IS BEING REMODELED!" However, if you have to live in the project, here are Nancy's survival tips: "plan and organize before starting. Know where things (like furniture, files, appliances, and tools) will be during the construction phase and plan for a longer span of time than told. Also, get everything in writing so it stays on a time-managed schedule."

Being TimeSmart
Turn Your Thoughts to Tools

I. Identify TimeSmart ideas of your own that are inspired by this chapter.

II. Solution seeking
1. Identify a productivity sapping challenge you occasionally face.

2. If you could change it from challenge to ideal, what would ideal be like?

3. Put check marks next to 3 ideas in this chapter that can help you successfully overcome the challenge.

4. Identify action steps to change the situation for the better and indicate when you will start each one.

Chapter V
Good-bye Procrastination, Hello Accomplishment

Not everything that is faced can be changed,
but nothing can be changed until it is faced.
JAMES BALDWIN

Small deeds done are better than
great deeds planned.
PETER MARSHALL

Do it NOW, Relax Later

Allison Foreman is a benefits coordinator living in Riverdale, GA. "One way that I manage time at home," says Allison, "is to start my chores *as soon as I get home*. I know that if I sit down and relax it will take longer to get things done because I will have to wake my body up. If I just go ahead and do them and get them out of the way, I get a lot done and have more time to relax for the evening."

Shifting Mental Gears as You Transition from Work to Home

"The things that I need to do at home I put on a to do list I keep at work," Johnny Jones, an information systems manager in Oklahoma City tells us. "As I am finishing up at work and prioritizing for the next work day, I also review the things that I need to do at home. So, on the way home from work I plan how I will accomplish my jobs at home."

Give It a One — Two Punch

Dave Lewis of San Diego, an engineer, reminds us that a way to get past putting something off is to just hit it with a double punch combination. First, "get everything needed for a job so when you get time for it, you're ready." Second, "think of all the reasons you haven't already done the job, then think how to fix each one."

Sweetening the Job

"When doing a semi-unpleasant task (such as writing checks to pay bills), I listen to music or watch music videos. This is relaxing and visually stimulating and promotes motivation to complete the task," says Sharon Peterson, a mental health worker in Sacramento, CA.

Small Increments Add Up

As an events coordinator, Lisa Ramirez of Burlingame, CA knows projects that are overwhelming are best done in pieces. "I break up large tasks into smaller increments," Lisa tells us. "For example, instead of sitting down at the end of the month for three hours to pay all my bills, I spend five minutes at a time to pay them as they come in. The same goes for housecleaning, I never do it all in one day. Monday morning before work I spend five minutes cleaning the sink, Monday evening when I get home I spend ten minutes cleaning the tub, etc."

Couch Potato Syndrome

"My tip for personal accomplishments," starts Carmen Nicoll of Pekin, IL, "results from my love of the *couch potato syndrome*. I break big tasks into four minute steps, then get up during commercials and tackle projects one step at a time. That way, you 1) don't endure the same advertisement several times throughout the evening, 2) accomplish goals, and 3) still catch favorite programs."

Deputize Your Children

One way to get over procrastination is to make ourselves accountable to other people. For example, if I tell Gayle I am going to paint the swing on Saturday or clean the garage on Sunday, I do not feel that I have any choice now but to dive into the promised jobs. Bruce Truxall of Columbus, OH employs the same concept.

"When I find myself avoiding a job I know I should do," Bruce informs us, "I tell my three year old son that he must help me get _____ done (or fixed). I know he will bug me about it until we do it together. The job gets done, we have a great time together, and we both learn something."

A Summer List

"Late spring or early summer," recommends Betty Lawson of Rochester, IL, who works for the Illinois State Police, "make a list of everything you would like to accomplish during warm weather. Each weekend or evening of choice do the one you most feel in the mood to do and mark it off the list. Keep the whole list so you can see how much you have accomplished."

One a Day

Lori Beagles of Springfield, IL also works for the Illinois State Police and also finds success over the urge to procrastinate by following the steady and sure route. "I try to choose one job I need to accomplish each day," says Lori, "such as catching up on filing, cleaning out one drawer, or something like that. And I get it completed. That way I have achieved seven non-routine tasks each week. I'm not overwhelmed with juggling all my spring cleaning all at once."

A Simple Plan of Attack

As a special events coordinator, Theresa Hutton, of Shepherdstown, WV, has a special knack for getting the job completed. She says, "I get things done at home by following this three step process:

1. Plan by making a list of to do's.
2. Set up time frames to do the above.
3. After completion I reward myself with a special treat (such as dinner out, or a manicure) in the evening."

Start

"If you are feeling overwhelmed just do something… anything," advises secretary Valerie Wilson of Dale City, VA. "Once you get started, its very easy to continue and begin to prioritize as you go. You'll see improvement and this will inspire you to continue."

Pick a Card to Beat Procrastination

Vikki Dullinger of St. Cloud, MN has an interesting idea for job roulette. "Put lists of tasks on 3 x 5 cards (assuming priorities are equal), then draw the next task out of a hat. It keeps a sense of chance alive and the routine doesn't get boring. This works well with household tasks and getting kids to do things. For kids you can add a suggested time to accomplish the task then have them try to beat it."

Just Do Ten

When she doesn't feel like doing something, Audrey Miller of Charlotte, NC psychs herself into starting the disagreeable task. How? "This may not seem totally psychologically sound," explains Audrey, "but when I have something to do that I dread, like housework, especially washing dishes or straightening a room, I'll tell myself *just do ten dishes* or *ten things then you can stop.* Usually once I start I'll go ahead and complete the tasks. Sometimes I do have to keep telling myself *that was good, just do ten more* until it's done. Sometimes I only get the first ten done but at least that's better than none at all."

Choose a Distraction That's Less Distracting

"I used to have a problem getting housework or cooking started at home after working all day," claims head nurse Susan DiBiose of Columbia, SC, "so I cut *Oprah* off and turned on the radio."

Mix the Good with the Bad

"To accomplish priorities, I mix in fun things with chores. I like to mow the lawn so I pair it with hedge trimming, which I don't like. All through the day I couple likes with not so likable things to do. I am less tired at the end of these days and accomplish more." Sounds like Tyrus Branom of Decatur, GA has found a way to boost productivity and drop stress simultaneously.

Music Beats the Blues

Phyllis White has an attitude. And it sounds like a cool one for beating the procrastination blues. "I put the music on and set a timer for scheduled things to be done at home. I may even dance as I go about my chores. Usually I get done before I know it and I really feel good with all that I have accomplished." And Phyllis adds, "singing (I cannot carry a tune, but *so what?*) brightens my way through the chores. I have done this for years."

Batch the Nitpicky Jobs

As a project manager in a design firm, Jeff Pergl from Marietta, GA, knows how to handle the big stuff. But the little stuff at home? That used to be a pain. "I used to have a problem with small tasks such as picking up my shoes, changing light bulbs, and refilling the water bottle in the fridge," explains Jeff. "These tasks would build up around the house until I made the commitment to do each small task as it arose in my travels around the house. Now a trip from the bedroom may take three minutes instead of thirty seconds but things don't pile up anymore. And what's three minutes out of an hour? I don't even miss it." And the nagging burden of the nitpicky jobs is off his shoulders, too.

How to Eliminate a Major Distraction

The number one job of the television broadcast industry is to get us to watch. So, of course, TV is a tantalizing distraction that compels us to pay attention to it instead of focusing on getting things done. David Eppler, an advertising man in Minneapolis, MN has some refreshing advice that works well to curtail procrastination. "Kill your TV. Unplug your television and drag it to your neighbors," David implores. "Make them promise not to give it back for at least a week no matter how much you beg. Keep a log of all the things you do when you would normally be sitting in front of the TV. *After a couple of tries you learn to just turn it off.*" All we can add here is, amen!

Being TimeSmart
Turn Your Thoughts to Tools

I. Identify TimeSmart ideas of your own that are inspired by this chapter.

II. Solution seeking
    1. Identify a productivity sapping challenge you occasionally face.

    2. If you could change it from challenge to ideal, what would ideal be like?

    3. Put check marks next to 3 ideas in this chapter that can help you successfully overcome the challenge.

    4. Identify action steps to change the situation for the better and indicate when you will start each one.

Chapter VI
Slice & Dice
Meal Preparation Time

Everything I have I owe to spaghetti.
SOPHIA LOREN

30 Days of Meals

"I used to spend a tremendous amount of time making a menu, a shopping list and then grocery shopping," says Tracy Cavanah of Rock Hill, SC, the busy director of a day school. To slice that time significantly, Tracy says she put "thirty days of meals on the front of index cards and on the back I wrote all the ingredients I needed. Now I pick up the first seven cards and head to the store. [In one trip I buy] everything I need so I cut out extra trips to the store. Also, I spend less because I am not just buying without a plan. We don't have the same thing over and over. And I know when I wake up what I'm cooking when I get home — which reduces stress and frustration. The meals my family especially enjoys I put on more than one card [because] when I finish a card it goes in the back of the pile." Clever, huh? Tracy adds another benefit of this system, "it also leaves a menu for my family in case I'm late."

Menu Matrix

Denise Schreiber of Queenstown, MD works at the Aspen Institute, a "think tank" organization. A TimeSmart idea of Denise's for simplifying meal planning is a *menu matrix*. It works like this: "I set up an index card with eight columns; across the top is titled: Week/ Sunday / Monday / Tuesday / Wednesday / Thursday / Friday / Saturday. On each line under *week* I write the dates for the week. Each square is used to list the meal for that night." At a glance, Denise sees "what's for dinner each night. It makes meal planning easy. It also helps me to vary meals and to organize grocery shopping. These cards are kept from month to month since I find meals tend to be seasonal (for example, hot soups versus cold sandwiches)."

Dinner du Jour

Kelly Kurtz of Lunenburg, MA offers this TimeSmart idea: "make a dinner menu for the week and post it on the refrigerator. Then whoever comes in first can start dinner. Plus this eliminates the nagging question, *what's for dinner?*"

Dinner du Jour

Try Ready-to-Eat

"As a single working mother," Mickey Mahon of Irmo, SC tells us, "I juggle work, school for my two girls, and going back to college. Ready-to-eat meals [from the store], although somewhat expensive, are a great time saver." And to justify the cost, Mickey notes "on nights there is school or kids' programs, we don't have the expense of going out to eat."

Thelma Jefferies puts her own spin on the idea of ready-to-eat. She writes, "I'm a single mother with two active children. I have a full time job and a part time job which consists of fifteen hours a week. I get involved with my children's activities — my son is a freshman in college and he plays basketball; my daughter is a freshman in high school and she plays basketball and runs track. [To maximize my time] I make a weekly meal plan and I cook all the meats for the week on Sundays and freeze them. During the week all I need to cook daily is the vegetables."

And Daffney Chang of Buford, GA adds, "for time management, my idea is to cook all meat foods in advance and freeze them." Daffney, however, cooks "for the month." The benefit to her? "I can spend more time with my family," she says. And less time with the oven, we say.

Sunday Cooking Dices Cooking Time the Other 6 Days

"Being that couples never have the time or feel like cooking after long hours," observes Angela Belanger or Nashville, TN, "we cook big meals on the weekends and freeze portions of beans, sauces, and soups. When we come home in the evening, we defrost the main entree and just cook rice and vegetables to go with it. This system works wonderfully. It is less expensive than going out to eat and usually healthier for us."

Rick Swiggett's family in Chillicothe, OH, also knows the value of preparing meals ahead of time. Rick says, "my wife, Toni, our 6 year old twins, and I spend four hours on Saturday afternoons and make the next week's dinners. All I have to do," continues Rick, "is heat things up and dinner is done by the time Toni gets home." And another benefit of this cooking strategy: "we have a great deal more evening time."

Index Card Menus

"I have a set of index cards with complete menus for regular family meals," writes Thea Suzy Hunt of Brandon, FL. A believer in being prepared, "I have an *emergency set* of cards for when guests show up at the last minute and I always keep emergency items on a specific pantry shelf." But what if a bus load of guests show up at the last minute? "I also have the numbers of several delivery restaurants."

Thea has a penchant for organization and also offers this TimeSmart tip for making a trip to the grocery store a ride in the fast lane. She tells us, "I made a master list of items I routinely purchase. I went to my store [so I could] put the list in order by aisle. Then I photo copied it. As I run out, I simply mark the items" and have a ready made shopping list.

Delegate to a Crockpot

Wilma Sheffer of St. Louis, MO appreciates letting "someone else" slowly cook the meal at home while she fast tracks at work. When we said this book would have a chapter in it about cooking and time management, Wilma passed this note to Doug, "don't forget to add the value of a crockpot for healthy meals ready to eat when you get home."

Get a Bigger Measurer

"Time saver for at home: instead of dipping out ten measures of coffee for a ten cup pot, measure out ten measures in a ½ cup measure or other vessel and use that amount to make coffee with one scoop!" suggests Elinor Pfluger of Indianapolis, IN. "Saves time everyday," she adds.

Buying Ready-to-Eat Is Not Cheating

"I often tell everyone who comes to my house that our home could really use a stay-at-home wife," confesses Carol Kelcher of Berrien Springs, MI. "Both my husband and I are university professors and we have two teenage children. I've finally come to the place where I realized I can't do it all. When entertaining I shop for a yummy ready-to-eat entree and maybe other major time consuming preparation items. I take the food out of the foil containers and plop it into a casserole or one of my personalized serving dishes. Most of the time no one knows the difference. If they ask for my recipe, I tell them, and we all have a great laugh. They appreciate not having to take the time to write the recipe down. They know where to go get it! We all save time!"

Feeding the Family Efficiently

Annette Butler of Fairmont Heights, MD has some suggestions for streamlining the meal process: "plan menus a week ahead of time and stick to them," she offers. "Include two or three quick meals such as tuna sandwiches and chips with possibly no leftovers. And two to three meals, including desert, with enough leftovers. Fridays everyone is on their own (for the little ones, McDonalds). Use paper plates and cups except on Sunday."

Cooking with Assistance

Around our house, everyone seems to drift in and out of the kitchen during cooking time. And since our two children, Amanda and Jimmy, are both teenagers, Gayle and I have gotten casual about leaving things cooking while we go for a walk together or read the newspaper on the front steps with a glass of wine; we just request, loud enough to be heard through the whole house, *turn the oven off in 20 minutes, we're going outside!*

Most of the time it works. However, sometimes the notion of 20 minutes gets hazy and the checker is left wondering *is it 20 minutes yet?* Amanda has come up with a great way to know exactly when the oven needs to be turned off, a roast turned, or the rice stirred. "Keep a small pad of

Post-it Notes in the kitchen," she recommends. "If you are going to leave the room and need someone else to do something, they can easily remember what you want them to do because the note says 'turn the oven off at 5:30' or whatever. Since I like to get several things going at the same time, like make a pie while the roast is cooking and broccoli is microwaved, I write notes to myself about what time to take stuff out of the oven. I stick them to the door of the oven so they remind me while I am doing other things."

Down Home Cooking Ideas

"Our lives are very full," says Barbara Harned of Tuscola, IL, an active wife and mother with two children under 5. "I cook extra meals on the weekends or during the week and freeze the food. I also cook a lot in the fall when I have days off from work. I will prepare and freeze several meat loaves, quiches, chilis, stews, and breakfast muffins in the late fall. We also use the crockpot a great deal. When cooking, I always clean my mess and wash what dishes I use as I cook. It helps avoid larger messes at the end of the meal. While one of us is cooking the other is teaching or playing with the children."

What Do We Need?

In New Orleans, where I was born and Gayle came to live as my bride, the local phrase for going to the grocery is *I'm making groceries*, as in, "I'm making groceries at Schwegmanns this afternoon. What do we need?" No

What Do We Need?

matter where you live, a time consuming part of meal preparation is shopping for the food and supplies. To cut the time, try these TimeSmart ideas for *making groceries.*

"To save time," reports Teresa Pass of Lebanon, TN, "I use a typed list of typical items I buy (be sure to leave room for adding new items). I organize the list of items according to my grocery store aisles. Also, when organizing coupons, I do it the same way — organize them according to the store's aisles. When I shop, it makes it easier and quicker."

Danna Dolliver has a clever tip that takes only minutes to do and frees up hours for doing more productive (and fun) things than grocery shopping. Thanks, Danna, for sharing these smart ideas with us: "I go grocery shopping once a week. And I save my receipt from the previous week. This shows all of the *basics* that I need to buy that week. During the next week, I turn it over and write down all of the *extras* for the next trip. This saves on the time it takes to write a whole new long list, plus I save time by not having to go back to the store several times a week for forgotten items."

Being TimeSmart
Turn Your Thoughts to Tools

I. Identify TimeSmart ideas of your own that are inspired by this chapter.

II. Solution seeking
    1. Identify a productivity sapping challenge you occasionally face.

    2. If you could change it from challenge to ideal, what would ideal be like?

    3. Put check marks next to 3 ideas in this chapter that can help you successfully overcome the challenge.

    4. Identify action steps to change the situation for the better and indicate when you will start each one.

Chapter VII
There's More to Life than Cleaning

Cleaning Time *Is* Quality Time

Betty Roebuck of Jacksonville, FL tells us, "spending time with my granddaughter is very important to me. However, it is hard to do laundry, clean house, and spend time with a seven month old baby. Doing laundry, I put the baby in her safety seat on top of the washer. She loves the spin cycle. Cleaning base boards, I crawl on the floor with her and clean at the same time. Vacuuming: (this is tricky) baby seat with suction cups on top of canister vac gives her a ride while I am working. We make cleaning house fun and we get to spend time with each other."

Multiply Your Time with Machines

"Teaching my teenage daughter the art of house cleaning and time management, our motto became: *if the washing machine, clothes dryer, or dishwasher are not operating while you are vacuuming the house, you are not managing your time well.* Use your stove clock timer to remind you of when to change your washer and dryer loads," recommends Patty Belvin, an administrative support assistant in Newport News, VA.

Whole House Deep Cleaning

Tracy Gorman of Florissant, MO has total quality cleaning down to a science and she shares her secrets when she says, "start at the back of the house. Carry a caddie full of cleaning supplies, a vacuum cleaner, and some empty plastic grocery bags with you (you might want a separate bag for each room; laundry baskets work, too). Clean each room completely, including the vacuuming, before you exit the room. If there are items in a room that belong in another room, put them in a bag until you get to that room. Cross the hall to the next room and repeat the procedure. Cutting out all of the time [and miles] you normally spend running back and forth, will save you lots of time!

Cluster Cleaning

Amy Parsons of Piketon, OH recommends moving things through the house in clusters. "When I get home from work," says Amy, it seems like "things always need to be put away in various parts of the house. When I need to go to the bedroom I will take everything from the other rooms that goes there, so I'm not making 100 trips to the bedroom every night. On my way out I'll bring the laundry and other stuff that goes elsewhere. So this way I'll only have to make one trip there per night."

Create a Laundry Dream Team

"Laundry was a problem consuming around 50% of my housework time," reports Cathy Bailey of Dryden, VA. "Now each member of our five member family has their own hamper for their laundry. Each member is charged with doing their own wash as they need it." The end result of this arrangement — "a big reduction in my laundry time." Plus, Cathy says *she* is responsible for the communal wash, like towels and sheets.

Wash Body & Clothes Together — Cuts Time

Tom Ewing of Heath, OH writes, "I am single and without a washer. My shirts and pants go to the cleaners. I am left with my shorts and socks. These go into the tub and are stomped as I shower. Two showers and they are clean."

Cut Down on Folding and Ironing

"Instead of being overwhelmed with loads of laundry and plenty of folding and ironing on the weekend, try this," suggests Karen Harrington of Inver Grove Heights, MN. "Wash shirts, throw them in the dryer for a few minutes, then take them out and put on hangers immediately. No folding or ironing needed."

Sandy Kelly of Peoria Heights, IL is an applications analyst at Caterpillar. Sandy recommends cutting down on folding and ironing time like this: "don't fold sheets after laundering. You're wasting your time. Instead, immediately put them back on the bed."

Swan Lake Redux

Maria Williams, an international sales coordinator in Oklahoma City, possesses rhythm, style, and imagination! "To polish wood floors and exercise at the same time," says Maria, "make booties out of old towels or diapers, soak them in oil, put on some fast music, and start moving!"

Start with a Pan of Dishwater

"Whenever I begin cooking or cleaning, I start a pan of dishwater so I can soak dishes as I go along," says Judith Randall of Norman, OK. "Also, if I have to bake and clean, I prepare food first and clean while it is cooking!" Judith can't resist; she adds this friendly reminder, "just remember to set a timer. Once I took a nap and the smell of burning woke me!"

Swan Lake Redux

Uncluttered Weekends

"As a full time employee who hates to spend any part of
the weekend cleaning house, I do it on Friday," Angela
Sheffer of Oklahoma City informs us. "I requested my
hours be flexible so I can leave early on Friday afternoons.
I limit myself to no more than three hours of housework.
By doing this, my husband and I are able to enjoy the
whole weekend. I also offer flextime to my employees."

Split the Work in Two

Heather Riley of Fenton, MO did not tell us her occupa-
tion but we are guessing marriage counselor. Heather
recommends, "choose a day of the week and split the
chores with your spouse. For example, one does the
vacuuming and bathrooms and the other does the dusting and kitchen. He does his laundry and I do mine."

Hang the Laundry

"If I am pressed for time and I have done laundry and
do not have time for the dryer," says Tish Landry, a
restaurant manager, full time student, and mother,
living in San Diego, CA, "I hang my damp clothes on
hangers until I can find time to throw them in the dryer
to soften them up."

Shortcuts Create a Relaxing Evening

Cindy Dye, from Kingsport, TN, a secretary in a hospital lab writes, "I have a small child. When I went back to work after maternity leave, I just about went NUTS! I never got to sit down during the evening and my weekends were nothing but work around the house. One thing I now do is get up a few minutes early and put a load of laundry in the washer and transfer the load already in the washer to the dryer. The first thing I do when I get in from work, I put the load I washed in the morning into the dryer. If needed, I wash one (and only one) load that night." To better use her cleaning time, Cindy also says she sets "aside two nights a week to clean different parts of the house. I have also set aside two nights to watch my favorite TV shows. We put a TV in the kitchen so I won't miss my shows if dinner is running late." Is all of this coordinated effort worthwhile? Cindy says, "by separating these duties, I have found my weekends are no longer all work and I enjoy my weekends with my family." Cindy also adds one more tip, if you schedule your washing and drying in a way that means wet clothes are left in the washer for a long time, "be sure not to do this with clothing that will bleed onto other clothes." That sounds like the voice of experience, doesn't it?

Stop Searching for the Next Plastic Bag

"When changing plastic liners in home wastebaskets, place several of the baggies unopened on the bottom," suggests Richard Albano of Northampton, MA. "Then place the open baggie to line basket. When changing the liners, pull out the old and then remove one of those on the bottom and line the basket without having to go to the cupboard. Use a rubber band to keep liner from sliding into the basket."

Schedule Housework Like Business Appointments

Michelle Gibson lives in Gaithersburg, MD and is an Assistant Director in the Chamber of Commerce. Michelle writes, "working ten to 12 hours a day and being a competitive ballroom dancer, I have had to organize the way I get things done at home. I have specific days for specific tasks. Saturdays I do laundry, Sunday I pick up the weekly clutter, Tuesdays I vacuum, Wednesdays I clean the cat box and so on. Also, regardless of my daily activities, I reserve 10 to 11 p.m. each week night for me to write letters, crochet, sew, take a bubble bath, or whatever I need."

Avoid the Clutter Flood

"I drilled into my three children to put things away as they are used," says U.S. Army training coordinator, Shirley A. Gervais. Some suggestions: "pick up things as you walk through a room on the way to somewhere else. Hang up coats when you come in. Throw away newspapers when read. Keep all loose items in zip lock bags. Take the trash out on the way out. Make the bed when you are getting dressed." All sensible advice for later avoiding the common problem of drowning in clutter.

Delegation

"Delegation," writes Darlene Kreiling of Philips, WI. "It took me many years of being a full time working mother and wife before I realized, I did not have to do everything. My teenage sons do their own laundry after *the straw broke the camel's back* when they needed jeans for school the next day — and it was 11 p.m.! The dirty jeans had been under their beds, of course! You need to realize you cannot do everything yourself, but the main thing to remember is that you also need to expect their effort. Remember the only way to get things right may be to do it yourself, but the way to get everything done is to delegate."

Coordinate the Efforts

Michael Davis, a computer whiz in Marietta, GA, admits, "I used to have a problem managing household chores. I have two roommates and the problem was that when one person was ready to do some cleaning the others were away." To remedy the challenge "what we do now is for thirty minutes a day, every day, all three of us clean one room. We have five rooms plus the kitchen and yard. And no, it never seems like we spend the whole weekend cleaning."

Cleaning Good Enough for Guests

"I try to have overnight guests at least every four to six weeks because it forces me to look at my house the way strangers would. And therefore, I have to clean with this in mind," reports Sarah Abood, a nutrition scientist at Ralston Purina. "Also, my husband always cleans the bathrooms so thoroughly!"

A Bed as Pretty as in the Magazine Pictures

Problem: Making the bed perfectly every morning.

Solution: Buy a down comforter. It takes less time and besides, it will never be *perfect* so you don't have to spend time trying to make it so.

This observation comes from Leslie Sharp of Atlanta, GA.

Let the Music Set Your Pace

She didn't tell us what it is, but Linda Bennett of Marietta, GA admits, "I used to have a problem getting a certain task done." Why? It was "do to [my] leisurely performing it like it was the only task or the very last task of my life. To increase the sense of urgency I set a timer at the estimated time of completion. Knowing that I have a designated time makes me work more diligently. Also, playing an album/CD with the goal of completion being the end of the last song on it helps to increase the sense of urgency. When I accomplish my goals, I often reward myself."

No Time to Clean? Try 4 a.m.

"I used to have a problem with finding the time for cleaning up when I got home from work, reports Tenjurie Thomas. "As I had other important things to do during the evening (like working late, exercising, running errands, choir rehearsal or committee meetings) I didn't have time for household chores. Now when I get home from those activities I go directly to bed. I wake up at 4:00 a.m. to clean up, wash clothes, wash dishes and organize my home. At this time in the morning there is nothing else to do. I'm not spending valuable time during business hours to do chores. This also helps me get an early start to work. I usually end up getting to work early and my day goes smoother."

Being TimeSmart
Turn Your Thoughts to Tools

I. Identify TimeSmart ideas of your own that are inspired by this chapter.

II. Solution seeking
   1. Identify a productivity sapping challenge you occasionally face.

   2. If you could change it from challenge to ideal, what would ideal be like?

   3. Put check marks next to 3 ideas in this chapter that can help you successfully overcome the challenge.

   4. Identify action steps to change the situation for the better and indicate when you will start each one.

Chapter VIII
Communicating with Love so Everyone's Singing the Same Song

When you look for the good in others
you discover the best in yourself.
MARTIN WALSH

Set Aside Time for Each Other

Peggy Mason of Aragon, GA appreciates the importance of communication with her spouse. "I make it a
practice," Peggy says, "to set aside at least one hour as
soon as I come in from work to converse with my husband about his day. In a very fast paced business world,
I think it's important to remember that family and
family communication is the stem of all success. I want
to make sure that he knows his well being and feelings
are important to me."

On the Same Wavelength

A relationship is a partnership. Obviously, more can
be accomplished and quicker when the partners act in
conjunction with each other. Erin Cheney of Gahanna,
OH explains how it works in her house. "We make
sure we have the same goals! Throughout the week we
talk about things that we need to do. For example, on
the weekend we make a to do list. Sometimes in order
to get the list done we have to do things separately
(example: he brings the car in, I do some flower gardening before company arrives). As long as we know each
others goals and are on the same wavelength, our to dos
get accomplished in a timely fashion! Then we have
more time for each other."

Woody Milley of Apalachicola, FL knows how two
people can get on the same wavelength and stay there
because they understand each other well. Woody says,
"my wife and I periodically swap job roles."

How to Keep Work from Infringing on Family Time

"My husband and I both check our work issues at the
door of our home," explains Susan Albicker of
Woodbridge, VA. Once we get home, we do not discuss
work or work issues, no matter how hard of a day we've
had. We focus on our family needs: getting dinner
ready, walking the dog, homework, and pre-bedtime
activities with our daughters. All work related items are
discussed or handled after the kids are in bed, usually 9
p.m. We've found that by focusing on our family life,

we are more relaxed and productive when we finally address the work related issues we've brought home. It also demonstrates our priorities to our daughters: that family is most important and our careers are important, but second."

Initial the Calendar

<u>Problem</u>: Your spouse says *you didn't tell me about that event*. You know you did.

<u>Solution</u>: Person with event or thing to do puts it on calendar and must then show it to other person involved and have them initial it to acknowledge the event. They can never say *you didn't tell me about that*. (And, if it's not initialed, you forgot to tell them.)

This advice was submitted by Don Jessen of Mt. Prospect, IL.

Synchronize Organizers

Computer analyst David Felts of Bristol, TN offers this tip for precise communication and focus on getting the right things done at the right time. "All of my family carries organizers, including my 8 year old daughter," says David. "We meet Sunday evening to plan the week synchronizing our calendars. This sets expectations and reduces conflicts plus teaches our child team skills."

Reading Together Shares More than Knowledge

"To put a positive conclusion to a hectic day," says Randy Croper of Elkhart, IN, "I lay down on our bed with both my daughters and my wife and read Bible stories from their Bibles. I also let the girls choose a prayer from their prayer book. We do this every night, no matter what the time or what we have done that day. Somehow, nothing is more soothing and comforting than reading a simplified child's Bible story with my family."

Comparing Calendars

Don Lambert of West Lafayette, IN says, "my wife (Sue) and I use our daily planners for communication of family information. We have a periodic family business meeting where we discuss current financial status, unusual bills, to do lists, car maintenance, appliance needs, child-proofing opportunities, picture taking, journal writing, and unnecessary inconveniences we do to each other. We also compare calendars for upcoming events, birthdays and anniversaries, and who is responsible for the card and gifts."

Family Pow Wow

"We have a 7 year old girl and a 9 year old boy. Both are very active and involved in sports, dance, you name it," reports Thomas Etter, a Captain in the U.S. Navy. "Working out a way to get everyone to all the activities in time plus have time to have the family at meals was

Comparing Calendars

problematic at best. We instituted a weekly *pow wow*. My wife and I work out an agenda ahead of time. At the meeting we routinely review minutes from the last meeting, everyone gets to give *an attaboy* [public praise] for the family, followed by a bug (what's bothering you). Next we discuss short range plans and schedules. We work out specifically who, what, when, and where for all activities for everyone in the family. This schedule is laid out on a large white board and then transcribed into our day planners. This process is repeated for long range single event planning such as vacations. The *pow wow* is closed with allowances for the kids that are somewhat dependent in how good a job they did that week accomplishing their chores. The outcome is a well organized map that coordinates all of our activities for the week. This allows everyone to be where they need to be in time, ready for the event, and to find time to sit down as a family and have meals together."

Exercise with the Kids

Ann Knudsen of Stillwater, MN, who works as a communications specialist, has a special forum for communicating with her children. "As a parent working full time," writes Ann, "I was struggling to fit my exercise time into my schedule and still leave room for blocks of time in the evening to focus on my children. The solution was to simply combine these two values. One or both children now accompanies me on a 45 minute brisk walk at least three evenings a week, in fact they compete over who gets to go with me. I love it!

Some of our best conversations take place on 'mom's walk' and I'm modeling the exercise habit for my children. This combines my personal exercise goals, quality time and conversation with the kids, and good parenting through modeling a healthful habit."

Enjoy Healthy Walks Together

Chris Woodbury lives in Clarence Center, NY and works as a social worker and family counselor. Chris shares a neat exercise tip for both physical and mental health: "my husband and I began taking evening walks about two years ago. Our dog goes, too, and he is very persistent about reminding us when it's walk time, so we never skip an evening. We walk 45 to 60 minutes. And besides exercise, it gives us a time... to talk, unwind, enjoy being outdoors, or simply enjoy being together. And of course the dog loves it."

So, Where Will Everyone Be?

"Sunday nights," L.A. MacEvoy of Gasport, NY writes: "our family has a family meeting, and the week is planned out — who gets out of school when; sports practices run from when to when; and who needs to get picked up when? Weekend activities are also included. Everyone in our family has an idea where each other will be and when so if something goes awry, the family can respond 'with ease.'"

It's Okay to Lean on Others

Ora Way of Jacksonville, FL appreciates that no one
achieves much by facing the world alone. Ora tells us,
"I am able to accomplish more since I have allowed my
circle of support to become active in my life. For years,
my parents and other relatives offered to assist me with
my responsibilities as a working wife and mother, such as
picking up the kids from school, preparing meals, and
providing sitter and respite care. However, I always said
no thank you because I felt that I had to do it [all myself].
All of our lives are more enriched by working together.
Working together provides gratification for all with a
favorable outcome. And they feel better helping me."

**Being TimeSmart
Turn Your Thoughts to Tools**

*I. Identify TimeSmart ideas of your own that are
inspired by this chapter.*

II. Solution seeking
   *1. Identify a productivity sapping challenge you
occasionally face.*

   *2. If you could change it from challenge to ideal,
what would ideal be like?*

   *3. Put check marks next to 3 ideas in this chapter
that can help you successfully overcome the challenge.*

   *4. Identify action steps to change the situation for
the better and indicate when you will start each one.*

Chapter IX
Homework & Housework: Raising Productive Kids (& Significant Others, Too!)

Happiness is a direction, not a place.
SYDNEY J. HARRIS

Share Responsibilities

"My husband and I have two young children," says Alice Bomar of Spartanburg, SC. "As a working mother I found it difficult to come home, bathe the children, help with homework, prepare dinner, and get ready for the next day. I have a loving husband and we discussed the problem. There are no hard and fast rules, but here's our plan. My husband, David, picks up our younger son and I pick up our older son. When I get home I prepare dinner while David supervises homework. David cleans up after dinner while I rest. Our older son gets out his clothes for the next day and bedclothes and towels for both boys. On Monday, Tuesday and Wednesday David

bathes the children. I bathe them the rest of the week.
Once a week we go out to dinner. I love this plan and
my family is organized."

Planning is Part of the Family Routine

"Get your children involved in planning family activities,"
suggests Susan Bevill, a computer whiz in Jacksonville,
FL. "Complete all house chores by Thursday night," says
Susan, "in order to go to the movies, bowling, or other
activity on Friday or Saturday. This helps your children
learn to plan and organize, as well as receiving rewards.
Praise and compliment your children as you would want
to be on your job."

Job Calendar Shows Who Will Do What & by When

"I have four teenagers and household chores are divided
among them. I keep a calendar posted on the refrigerator
listing the chore and who is responsible for it," notes
Benjamin Stillwell, a maintenance supervisor in Jacksonville, FL. "The assignments are rotated weekly so no one
person is stuck with an undesired task. Also, family meetings are called as needed to discuss major happenings such
as vacation plans and school schedules. Input is received
from all members of the family in regard to the best way
to achieve the goal discussed. Sometimes we discuss the
household chore calendar. Input in this area certainly helps
with chore attitude and I find I need to supervise less."

Lonnie's Keys to Raising Children

Lonnie Scott of Elkhart, IN shares this wisdom for bringing up great kids. Her keys to raising children are:

"1. Love them.
2. Listen to their thoughts and concerns.
3. Provide for them.
4. Teach them to respect the rights of others.
5. Teach them right from wrong.
6. Make sure they get an education."

Job List

"Being a mother of four," says bank teller Linda Jones of Jacksonville, FL, "I found making a job list for the week works well. Whether the child is three or 18, it gives them a sense of worth. We rotate jobs each week. They are given out according to age of the child. After two weeks, rewards are given, such as a special day somewhere (like the beach or movies) if all is accomplished."

How About a Marriage of Homework & Housework?

At the home of Wendy Fimbres of La Quinta, CA, it is clear cut: "with my kids," says Wendy, "to save time on arguing about homework and cleaning the house [they have a choice]. If they maintain a B average they don't have to do housework, just clean up after themselves. If the grade falls below B, they help with the work until it is back up."

Pre-match Outfits

Does too much of your morning time go into getting
clothes together for the children? Judy Lutzo of Abingdon,
VA has a solution. "Pre-match children's outfits for quick
dressing." One way to do this is alternate tops and bottoms
when you stack clothes. Each pair in the stack coordinates.
Judy also suggests using "large Ziplock bags for tops,
bottoms, socks and accessories such as a bow, ponytail
holder and jewelry."

Even Child/Odd Child

Terri Hood has a common sense, squabble-ending idea
that is so effective we are amazed everyone of us with
children does not automatically do it. Terri says, "I used to
have to referee fights in the morning between my grade
school children over who gets to sit in the front seat and
who sits in the back. One day we tried this: child #1 gets
the front seat on odd number days and child #2 on even
numbered days. What a charm! We no longer have fights
at the car and they can always tell mama what day of the
week it is."

Comfort in Schedules

Having a schedule can be comforting to young children.
Eliza Dorsey, a Fort Worth, TX math teacher tells us, "we
stick to our schedule as far as bedtime for the children.
They are trained so well! Regardless of where they are,
they go to sleep when it's their bedtime."

It Just Takes a Little Training

"I work nine to ten hours a day," writes Dannette Carson, a training coordinator who lives in Mount Holly, NC. "We have a 5 year old son. Coming home to do the dishes, laundry, dinners, and whatever else was not done felt impossible. I love to exercise, [but exercising is] not possible when your child wants to help you do aerobics while he brings his ten stuffed animals. Considering I am a trainer, I trained my husband to load the dishwasher, showed him some easy tips on cooking, and taught him how much bleach to put in the whites cycle. Now I can come home to a clean house with not dinner or clothes to do. And my aerobics is completed first thing before I go and get my child from daycare. I love having someone who shares my time and my duties."

It's Amazing What Ten Minutes a Day Can Do for Lifetime Memories

"Being a single full time working mother of two, I felt guilty not being able to spend special time with each child. We eat together most of the time and say our prayers at night. We kiss in passing. But I still needed the special time," says Trisa Yunis of Orangeburg, SC. "Now I get up early at 5 a.m., prepare myself for the day, and with twenty minutes to spare, I divide the time ten minutes for each child. I get in bed with each and it's my time to dedicate minutes solely to each one. I tell them how special they are, how much I love them, and shower them with affection. They have time to express their feelings without the other child intruding. My two children are wonderful. It's amazing what ten minutes a day can do for lifetime memories."

Children Can Help, Too

Kathy Kotecki is a customer service coordinator in LaSalle, IL and she knows the importance of getting the children involved in work at home. "Let your children help with chores," recommends Kathy, such as "cleaning windows, mirrors, dusting, putting your checks in order to help balance the checkbook, sorting laundry, and dressing the baby. It teaches them responsibility and saves you time."

Give Options to Get Agreement

"I learned this from my brother," says Vince Adelman of Perryville, MO. "When giving someone a challenge or assignment, always give them a choice of at least two things. This makes the challenge more acceptable; people like options. For example, instead of telling my son to clean up his room, I said, 'Derek (15), you need to either clean up your room or take out the garbage. Which would you rather do?'"

Read While Bathing

"While bathing my young son, we sing songs and I read to him while he plays with his toys in the tub. Now, I only have to read one book [to him] when he is in bed and we've had quality time," says Adrienne Fails, a middle school teacher living in Fort Worth, TX.

Give Options to Get Agreement

Brag Board

So often, people who see themselves as failures feel
they are unable to accomplish anything worthwhile.
Sandy Goodnight of Elkhart, IN is making certain her
children know they are winners and appreciate their
abilities for getting things done. "Being a working wife,
mother and part time college student, I struggled for a
way for my children to receive positive feedback on
their schoolwork," says Sandy. Simply posting school
papers on the refrigerator was insufficient because the
papers change each week. Something more comprehen-
sive was needed. "I made a *Brag Board* corkboard.
Each week, together, we pick out outstanding papers,
put congratulatory stickers on them, and tack them on
the board. No papers come down until the end of the
school year. This way they can see their mountain of
accomplishments. This takes only ten minutes each
week." And gives the kids a positive foundation for
believing in their abilities to get things done.

True Quality Time

We hear a lot about *quality time* with people we love.
Shirley Corbett of Jessup, MD reminds us that, "thirty
minutes doing what they want to do is closer bonding
than doing three hours of what you want to do."

Things Get Done by People

Richard F. Jubie is a project manager working for the County of York (VA). He employs his professional skills at home to both get the necessary chores accomplished and to teach his family skills for getting things done. "We develop task worksheets in different colors, one for each child, with the various tasks or household chores," Richard shares with us. "Children have to complete the last chores to obtain their weekly allowance. Also, there are bonus jobs (optional) with the goal of having the child pick their earned reward. We have a weekly family meeting to discuss weekly schedules, special concerns, and identify conflicts. All four of us have planners to note key events on the master schedule. We emphasize *things get done — or not done, by people.*"

Please Make Me Feel Important

One way to help the people around you stay productive is to appreciate their contribution. Geralyn MacDonnell of Rutland, MA, a supervisor of environmental studies, notes that we can "make believe that everyone you come in contact with has a sign around their neck that says *please make me feel important.* I keep this saying above my desk and try to incorporate it daily. You know the people who are in higher positions are always treated with the most respect and importance (at least to their faces). To be sincere to the lowest paid employee on the job, or to your family member (husband, wife, children, mother, etc.) makes them feel needed and important — which ultimately achieves results. This is… certainly what the family needs."

Bath Alternative

"With three kids and both parents working full time, it's very busy at our house in the evening," says Sally Martin, RN, of Arlington, TX. "To save 45 minutes to an hour, occasionally we skip our baths (the kids). Have the kids wash their face, armpits, and private parts with baby wipes or washcloths and change their underwear. They are clean and you've saved at least 45 minutes on bath time."

Time Management Habits Can Start Early

"Every morning," starts Tony Hall of Arlington, TX, "I encourage my young daughter to do the same three things in the morning so that she feels good [about herself]: use the bathroom, wash her face, and brush her teeth. She will run in the room to tell me that she is awake, she is done, and she is happy, because she knows that I am happy with her."

How to Get a Book Report Done *Fast*

"When my 9 year old son has a book report due tomorrow that he decided to tell me about tonight," points out Virginia Beach, VA resident Michelle Finklea, "I have him record his book on a tape recorder while I am nearby cooking. Later, he listens to his recorded story and answers the *five w's* (who, what, when, where, why). [While I get ready for bed] he reads the five sentences to me while I am behind the shower curtain in the tub. Together we get a healthy draft of a report, dinner, and preparations for bedtime in about three hours."

Getting the Right Things Done at the Right Time is Fun

Barbara Nickell of Brooklyn Center, MN knows that it is a team effort to run a household. What if the team members are very young? No matter. Barbara points out, "as a busy mom who works 40 hours a week, I would never get anything done at home if my children ages six and three didn't help. Of course first I had to lower my standards (children don't do jobs perfectly) and we had to make things fun to motivate them. We make up games. Also, we may compete: for example, my 6 year old will tidy the family room while I clean the kitchen and put the dishes in the dishwasher. He tries to finish first — but he can't just stash things, they have to be put away properly. The children have motivation (to beat mommy), it's fun (we love games), and after we finish we get some kind of reward (such as a book read or longer bath time)."

Bedtime Song

In some families, the children feel burdened by *having* to do something, even something as minor as getting ready for bed; in others, the job is made fun. The fun approach might make it easier for grown children to put the burdens of the adult work world into perspective. "Our family developed a routine with our girls," says Jill Anderson, RN, of Greenwood, IN. "Sara wasn't even 2 years old when we made up the *Jamie Time Song*:

Jamie time,
Jamie time,
Jam jam jamie time,
Jamie time,
Jamie time,
Jam jam jamie time,
Jamie...

This song was sung as dancing pj's flew into the bedroom after their baths. The girls, laughing, were clean, with pj's on, and ready for bed. Then off for prayers and quiet music. Bedtime was fun, the routine was established, and a family time was developed. Sara and Kate are thirteen and ten, but every now and then the *Jamie Time Song* comes up... remembered with smiles."

Gold Stars Work

"Get kids to pitch in," recommends Cheryl Zollars, a chief accountant who resides in the Columbus, OH area. "Create a simple chart with blocks. Each time kids help, they earn a star. After a number of stars are obtained — reward them."

Kids Want to Learn. Why Resist Nature?

Graphic Designer Carole Kincaid of Bexley, OH reminds us of the importance of letting little ones help us with the home jobs. "I have a 2 year old," Carole says, "who wants to do everything Mommy does and help with everything.

My son helps with chores at this early age when most parents say *no, you can't do that*, thinking the child is not old enough yet. I think children can and want to learn very early in life. My son vacuums all the rooms, dusts, cleans the glass tabletops, and feels so proud he can do these things with me. My cleaning time is reduced while developing a positive, nurturing relationship with my son."

Schedule the Details, Too

"I have four children. I also have a full time job plus a part time job teaching classes at local universities," reports Pamela Gatto Haring of Indianapolis, IN. "I make a schedule each day, for example: *Monday a.m. — children to school, fix lunch. Monday p.m. — Stephanie marching band 3:30-5:30 need to pick up. Diane cross country 4:00 to 6:00. Car pool by Mrs. Doe.* I plan each day with detailed information such as things needed to be taken, appointments, overnight stays, and parties. I post them on the door using different colored highlighter markers to help eliminate hassles and complications."

Being TimeSmart
Turn Your Thoughts to Tools

*I. Identify TimeSmart ideas of your own that are
inspired by this chapter.*

II. Solution seeking
   *1. Identify a productivity sapping challenge you
occasionally face.*

   *2. If you could change it from challenge to ideal,
what would ideal be like?*

   *3. Put check marks next to 3 ideas in this chapter
that can help you successfully overcome the challenge.*

   *4. Identify action steps to change the situation for
the better and indicate when you will start each one.*

Chapter X
Getting What You Want:
Going for the Goals

*The indispensable first step
to getting the things you want out of life is this:
decide what you want.*
BEN STEIN

*Unhappiness is not knowing what we want
and killing ourselves to get it.*
DON HEROLD

Focus on Tomorrow Tonight

Dave Bright, a quality control supervisor and engineer in Plymouth, IN, tells us, "I am a single divorced father raising three children ages 4, 9, and 12. To get organized, every night before going to bed I write the schedule for tomorrow."

Make a List

List making is an old-as-the-hills idea but it works.
Besides helping the memory, lists keep our minds
focused and not diverted by every loud noise or shinny
thing that tries to steal us away. "I always keep pen
and paper handy (in the car, purse, desk) and as things
come to my mind I write them down," says Connie
Lee Kastelic of Canal Winchester, OH. "At the house,
I keep a wipe-off board and write things there, too. I
try to condense all the lists into one and check off
items as I get them done."

Days Happen Automatically, Accomplishments Don't

To make certain you get the right things done at the right
time, do your personal version of what Karin Brady, a
sales representative living in Lawrenceville, GA, does:
"I plan daily goals, sometimes as little as grocery shopping and laundry. But every one is an accomplishment."

Sheila Gorham of Morrow, GA has similar success. "I find
I need the proper mind set to get anything accomplished,"
Sheila tells us. "I need to focus on a situation or task
mentally to define it, work through it in my mind, realize
what the results will be, and get to work." Which reminds
us of the theme of Napolean Hill's book, *Think and Grow
Rich*. Early in the twentieth century, Hill interviewed the
most financially successful businesspeople of his day. He
discovered a common thread that ran through their lives
was the deeply held belief that *if you can internally see it
and believe it, you can achieve it.*

Keep the Clock on Your Side

"To help me with my problem of running late," confesses office manager Betsy Davis of Columbia, SC, "I started setting my alarm clock fifteen minutes fast. I now set all clocks in the house and my watch ten to fifteen minutes fast. It works like a charm! I often get excited when I realize I have five minutes or so to spare. It's good to vary the change between ten to fifteen minutes so I'm never really sure which one it's at. That way I don't cheat. I have to assume its fifteen minutes."

Keep Pushing Forward

"Deal with problems. Do not be afraid to fail," advises Robert Richards of Sterling, MA. "Human nature is to pick yourself up and dust yourself off and start again!" We all know Robert is right. No matter what happens, life goes on and we should choose to employ our energy for forward movement. One of Doug's favorite quotes is from Kin Hubbard, "lots of folks confuse bad management with destiny." Keep moving forward and keep learning how to live a better life.

Stay Your Course

Sometimes people disrupt our focus and try to pull us in their direction. Scott Cooper of Virginia Beach, VA handles it well. At a seminar Doug taught, he handed Doug a piece of paper with words recalling an ancient wisdom: "nothing frustrates an angry man's intentions more than your calm in the face of adversity."

Future Focused

"My wife and I plan ahead. We write our long term
goals — usually 5 year and 20 year. We already plan
to live to 100 years old (we're in early 30's)," reports
Brian Garbera of Newark, OH. "Our short term goals
are based on our long term goals, so on Sunday we ask
each other what the week looks like and determine our
schedules. We also make sure that relaxing is on our
schedules. That way we can look forward and feel in
control because we have a plan. During the day, we'll
call each other to check our plans and adjust our
schedules if necessary."

Wish List for Achievement

Lisa Witherow of Westerville, OH, a training coordinator at Bath & Body Works, recommends, "begin your
day by writing a wish list that includes desired accomplishments. Review the list and rank them according to
level of importance (A,B,C). Then assign each task a
value based on level of difficulty (one being easiest and
five being the most difficult). For every task assigned a
value of three or above, break it down into action steps
for getting the task accomplished... Begin working
toward accomplishments based on first priority." The
rationale for doing it this way? Lisa points out, "making
a list of accomplishments rather than tasks is more
motivating. Also, assigning values based on difficulty
helps simplify the seemingly overwhelming tasks. And
breaking large or difficult tasks into smaller pieces
makes the accomplishment more approachable."

Triple To Do Lists

"In order to get things done at work or home, I usually have three to do lists. The first is for long term goals or projects, the second for relatively imminent ones, and the third for just the day's tasks. These apply to either things I have to buy or things I have to do. The mere fact of putting something on paper makes it seem half licked." This advice comes from mechanical engineer, Dan Sheffield, of Elmira, NY.

Run, Talk, and Plan

Certified Financial Planner, Tina Cirillo of Columbus, OH says, "I choose to begin each day with a long run. During my run I discuss my day with myself and what I want to accomplish that day. I then prioritize this in my mind. Later in the morning (not only at work, but for home also) I list these items in order and begin to tackle each one."

Keep Your Priorities in Sight

Insurance salesman Herman Dixon of Martinsburg, WV is noted for high productivity and his ability to get the right things done at the right time. His secret? "I make a list with timelines and deadlines and post them around the house so that they are in sight. I post them inside, on the refrigerator, at the back door, in the bathroom, on the TV remote, in our vehicles and in the bedroom. It keeps me focused and I get results."

Sandra Smith of Grove City, OH also find value in strategically placed reminders. "I put a Post-it Note on my kitchen cabinet door (on the outside) where I'll see it first thing in the morning or when I get home from work. On it are things that need to be done. Items accomplished are checked. When only a few remain, I start a new list."

Old Chinese Saying

Sheila Lemus of Greenbelt, MD takes heart during stressful times, smiles, and feels renewed when she thinks of this simple thought: *everyone excels in something in which another fails.* "This is my favorite Chinese fortune from a cookie," laughs Sheila, "however, I think a Chinese philosopher said it."

TimeSmart People are Strong

The stresses of daily life can potentially knock us off target. "I've spent three years in the throes of one personal tragedy after another," says Mindi Webster of Fredericksburg, VA, "plus, raising two toddlers and working a technical/professional part time job. During that time, we built a house, moved the family sixty-five miles and I took on more responsibility at work. I believe that I can achieve a high level of successful productivity because I:
1. stay organized
2. prioritize duties, responsibilities and needs
3. communicate well with spouse, boss and children
4. and challenge myself to reach beyond what's cozy."

Whiteboard Communication for Joint Focus

One person can run a rooming house, but it takes more than one to run a household. To stay in tune with each other in running their home, Wendy Buchman of Cortland, NY has this to say: "my husband and I list our home projects and items that need to get done around the house on a whiteboard that's magnetically attached to our refrigerator. We then try to complete the tasks before the marker used becomes semi-permanent and harder to erase! We feel a great sense of accomplishment when the whiteboard becomes clean and less covered with pen. It also helps us set goals and communicate with each other on things that need to get done."

A Quiet Space

Of course, for some of us, solitude is a requirement for achieving focus on how to handle something. Okay, but what if you live and work in perpetually tumultuous surroundings? "Go to the nearest public library," advises John David Church of Woodstock, GA. "The tables are big and the room is quiet. There is a pay phone but no phone that rings. They have a copy machine and the bathroom is clean." Plus you can behave like a kid in a brain candy store and taste a few treats. Says John, "after I work for 45 minutes [in the library], I'll treat myself to 15 minutes of reading something I wouldn't buy". Sounds like a good place to hang out when you want peace. And, John adds, "forty five minutes in the library is like three hours at the office."

Being TimeSmart
Turn Your Thoughts to Tools

I. Identify TimeSmart ideas of your own that are inspired by this chapter.

II. Solution seeking
   1. Identify a productivity sapping challenge you occasionally face.

   2. If you could change it from challenge to ideal, what would ideal be like?

   3. Put check marks next to 3 ideas in this chapter that can help you successfully overcome the challenge.

   4. Identify action steps to change the situation for the better and indicate when you will start each one.

Chapter XI
Home is No Place for Stress

*I don't know the secret to success
but the key to failure is to try to please everyone.*
BILL COSBY

*Plenty of people miss their share of happiness,
not because they never found it,
but because they didn't stop to enjoy it.*
W. FEATHER

Balance Between Personal and Professional Lives

Sometimes the line between work and our personal lives blurs. When you are in a key position in an unpredictable business (like health care, real estate sales, or the hospitality industry to name three), it is not always easy to say *no* when business intrudes on your personal life. "Many times I have to separate my professional life from my personal life," reports Lisa Berg of St. Petersberg, FL who works as Assistant Front Office Manager of a Hyatt Regency Hotel. "My significant other does not enjoy hearing about my troubles at work. So we made a pact — every time I complain about my stress from work or accept going in on a day we have [personal] plans, I owe him a quarter." Lisa says this has changed how she approaches her work. "I have learned to prioritize [better] at work and leave it. Not to mention I am less stressed."

Music Melts Stress

There is something about music that can not only melt stress but it also sparks us with energy. "I always make time everyday to enjoy listening to music and really listen to a whole tape or CD without interruption," says Jim Scicchitano of Woodstock, GA. "This for me, revives me and gets me in the frame of mind to get things done."

Clear the House Out

How does Andre Dennis of Atlanta, GA drop stress and stay sane? "I get rid of everyone in the house and take a little time to do something for me — read, TV, a treat, or a hot bath. Something that makes me feel good." Actress Greta Garbo meant sort of the same thing in the 1930's when she often murmured her signature line, "I want to be alone." Is there any greater luxury?

Read What Inspires You

"I read inspirational and devotional literature while waiting at the doctor's offices, or children's lessons," says home health care coordinator, Tami Donaldson of China Grove, NC. "This helps me to relax and become more focused the rest of the day, especially on busy days. Also, I listen to self-help tapes in the car while commuting."

Take 30 Minutes to Unwind

Many of us face a full day of responsibilities at work and then go home to face a full evening of responsibilities from our family. We love them, but sometimes they overwhelm us. Marcy Wiggins of Moore, OK says "I realized when I walked in the door at home that I was bombarded with questions, concerns, and wants from my family (husband and two children). This was very frustrating to me. About a year ago I began to declare a *time out*. When I walk in from work I say *hello* to let them know I am home, then I go directly to my room, close the door and turn on one of my favorite compact discs. For 20 to 30 minutes I am alone to collect my thoughts for the day with no questions, concerns, or wants addressed until I emerge from my room. This has been beneficial to both me and my family. They receive a lot more positive answers from me than they did before."

Isn't Life Too Short to Worry about What to Wear?

Sometimes a bit of extra attention at home avoids stress that might be brought into work. Mona Colbert of Naperville, IL says, "I've worked outside the home for over thirty years. On the weekend, Saturday or Sunday afternoon, I pick out five outfits that I'm going to wear the following week. I match the blouses to slacks then press them all making the necessary repairs and put them in a spare closet. Then at 6 a.m. on Monday morning I don't have to decide what to wear or face the *I don't have anything to wear syndrome*. I know it fits, is clean, needs no repair and I have no stress at the last minute."

Write Your Thoughts & Sleep Like a Baby

"I put a pen and pad beside my bed for those things to do that come up in the middle of the night," reports Susan Stroud, RN, of Kingsport, TN. "I can rest relieved that I don't have to keep it stored in my memory until morning. These tasks have a better chance of being completed and I don't take the time trying to recall several things at once."

Waiting for Your Child Can be Relaxing

"I change my clothes before leaving work," says Denise Calbert of Rantoul, IL, "while waiting to pick my son up from practice, I walk or jog around the track at his school until he's ready to go. If it rains I workout a little bit with weights. I use my time wisely by not going home and having to leave again to pick up my son."

Try Shifting Your Waking Hours

Frequently, Doug informs the people in his audiences about his latest writing project and asks for their personal input. W. Waterfield, MD of Mt. View, CA, gave him this note: "what I do to get things done — I go to bed an hour or two earlier and get up an hour or two earlier and get things done when my mind is most clear and I'm not tired and drained from my day's work." That sounds like a stress-dropping strategy to us.

Write Your Thoughts & Sleep Like a Baby

Relax by Learning to Trust Your Family More

"I was a stay-at-home mom for ten years before I went back to school and then began working full-time," Linda Freudenberger of Lexington, KY informs us. "It was very difficult to drop the *super mom* status. In order to manage my time more effectively I had to delegate jobs to family members and lower my standards, especially for the house cleaning. I'm still learning after three years. I had to do a big attitude change to lower my internal stress so I could function more effectively at work."

Put on Home Clothes Before You Leave Work

Mary Moreland of Ridgefarm, IL says, "I change clothes at work before I leave to go home. The results are I'm comfortable, I can begin making the transition from work to home, and I can jump right in when I get home. If I don't do this I lose about half an hour of home time because the demands of home (phone, kids, and supper) draw out the whole process."

Will It Matter in the Future?

Kerseinya Wentworth of Van Etten, NY is a psychiatric social worker. Kerseinya deals with her own stress like this: "when I start to get emotionally overwhelmed about projects and getting things done, I stop and ask myself, will this energy I'm diverting to this issue really matter in five years? in one year? tomorrow? If it's really no big deal, I let it go and don't get caught up in it."

It's Okay to Focus on *Me*

"I get up ten minutes early so I can read the paper and have a cup of coffee just for me. *Me* comes first in the morning because *me* manages the time that helps *me* manage deadlines all day. I can handle stress or anything that is thrown at me just by starting the day off with ten minutes for me. At night it's another 20 minutes just for me to finish the paper and relax before bed," says Janice Van Wormer of Sparta, WI.

Returning to Work after a Baby is Stressful

Financial analyst Laura Aniton of Reynoldsburg, OH shares this with us: "I work in a fast paced retail business environment and recently had a baby girl. Everyone said that I would want to quit my job — that it would be too much. But I'm here to say that it can work! At work, I make sure I manage my boss in that he knows my priorities. At 5:30, I leave. But I push to get everything done by then. I stay focused at work and think only about work (for the most part). Then when I get home, my career is put in the back of my mind and I concentrate on my family. I get a lot of support from my husband, which is the key."

Laura also offers a few tips on how she stays productive at work and home without becoming stressed.

"1. Use your daily planner, even at home.
2. Spend quality time with your husband and children until they go to bed. Then spend an hour getting daily things done.

3. Try to spend a half hour a day by yourself.

4. Use your driving time to think of things to do. Talk into a recorder to remember.

5. I keep three sets of baby things (like diapers, wipes, powder). One each in diaper bag, in the family room, and in the nursery.

6. Set a weekly goal — one different thing to clean or work on to get my spring cleaning done.

7. Bring your lunch to work and use your lunch hour for errands."

Jog to Work. Jog to Home

"My schedule is full, with a family and a full time professional career," says Monica Greens of Salinas, CA. "I found an apartment within ten minutes jogging distance from my office. This daily exercise helps me stay fit and reduces my stress level. My life is simpler and the environment, minus one commuter, is a little cleaner."

Keep Smiling

Sarah Tarr of Abilene, TX says, "a *laugh* a day, helps keep the doctor away." We believe she is right. A positive mental attitude is more than just trying to focus on the good. Positive people laugh. Isn't life full of inconsistencies and things that sometime do not work out like they should? TimeSmart people roll with the punches. Sarah throws in another beautifully simple thought, "smiles are contagious."

Ronae Allen of Fairfield, AL also offers up a thought to help us stay strong. "If something is not within your control," says Ronae, "don't worry about it. Clear your mind of that worry, replace it with something you can control and resolve."

Being TimeSmart
Turn Your Thoughts to Tools

I. Identify TimeSmart ideas of your own that are inspired by this chapter.

II. Solution seeking
    1. Identify a productivity sapping challenge you occasionally face.

    2. If you could change it from challenge to ideal, what would ideal be like?

    3. Put check marks next to 3 ideas in this chapter that can help you successfully overcome the challenge.

    4. Identify action steps to change the situation for the better and indicate when you will start each one.

Chapter XII
Smart "Little Ideas"
& the Last Word

It is kind of fun to do the impossible.
WALT DISNEY

Ode to Time Management

"After many years as a respiratory therapist," says
Renee Portmann of Fargo, ND, who is now successfully
developing a new career, "working all shifts and going
back to school, I have to guarantee to myself that on my
days off I will have free time to have some FUN." In
her own words, here are Renee's tips for using weekday
time efficiently to free up weekend time:

"1. I scrub the tub one or two times a week while
taking a shower.
    2. I get up one hour earlier in the summer to weed
and water my flower gardens.
    3. I spent three weeks cleaning my house of *every-
thing* that I had not used, worn, listened to, etc. in the

last 2 to 3 years. I donated it to charity. Now my house is *simplified* and I spend less time cleaning knick-knacks, moving things around, and *making room*.

4. I use my computer at home for *money management*!!!"

Go Cordless to Get More Done

"Thank goodness for the portable phone!" exclaims Lu Fleming of Norman, OK. "My daughter and I love to talk but I felt I was wasting time. I would never let her know that! Now I can talk, wash dishes (dishwasher), do laundry (washer and dryer), clean the oven (self cleaning), and pay bills all at the same time!"

TimeSmart Tips from Toni

Toni Thompson, an occupational therapist in Lutz, FL, shares some effective ideas for maximizing your time.

"1. I carry address labels to put on coupons, cards and forms I have to fill out.

2. Children's sports practices are good times to walk laps around the field, pay bills, write letters, write articles and to clean out the car.

3. It takes less time to change my own oil than it does to take the car in to the shop.

4. Having a gift box full of gifts that can be used for that forgotten or last minute birthday, holiday or house warming is a great time saver."

Read! Read! Read!

Welcome to the Information Age. Bob Miner of Tulsa, OK has thinking that is right in line with the new demands of our express-lane world. "As a professional," he points out, "I am always needing to read to stay current. I keep reading material with me all the time. Instead of sitting idly at a doctor's office, dentist's office, or waiting for someone, I read from sources that give me the information I need to stay current. The bottom line: turn idle time into productive time!"

Idle Time? Life's Too Short

Nurse Tina Holt of Ft. Worth, TX also makes full use of *idle time*. "When picking up kids, I clip coupons, catch up on correspondence, or do reading while waiting in front of school. To get one hour of walking a day for exercise, I put dinner in the oven on a low setting and go for my walk. When I get home, dinner is ready." This next tip from Tina is on a different subject but it is too good to edit out: "I buy everything in a different texture, for example white socks, so everyone can tell whose socks are whose without difficulty." The *little ideas* are usually the best!

Finding Lost Minutes

Elementary School Teacher Lisa Grundstrom of Bloomington, MN recommends you "be on the look out for lost minutes and make them productive. In making time for your personal life, use every lost minute. Some examples: talk to your children in the car; play word games; talk trivia; tell stories (a long lost art); show off points of interest in your own city. With training, you can find time to manage more effectively throughout your entire day." And have more fun!

Little Pieces of Spare Time Add Up to a Mountain of Productive Time

"I went to college part time while working full time. I still wonder how I fit everything in! But the biggest help was using all the spare time I had. Instead of chatting during lunch and breaks at work I used that time to read. It gave me an extra hour every day which added up to five hours per week. Totaling it up for one class that lasted fourteen weeks and I calculated I had *seventy hours extra* that I might have blown. This simple principle allowed me to get my degree and still have free time after class for a life in the process." Thanks to Diane Casper of Milwaukee, WI for this insight.

Reading Is Great, And There are Other Ways to Keep Up

"I always have reading material in my vehicle," says Mary Adams of Springfield, IL. "It's useful when waiting for the train or someone at the store, like when my husband or child runs into the store for a loaf of bread and takes twenty minutes. I make good use of my time. When I travel by myself I listen to tapes of books as

I prefer that to reading. When cleaning the kitchen or house, I try to have a news station on to keep up on current events without taking extra time to read about them." And we have to add a note here. Mary must have *efficiency* genetically coded in her genes; instead of searching for a sheet of paper, Mary sent her suggestions to us beautifully hand written on the back of a brown paper bag!

6 Ways to Maximize Your Time

In Oklahoma City, Kathy Lueb is an audit manager. Here are some of Kathy's thoughts on how she uses her time more efficiently.

"1. I have a maid service come in once a month to do the jobs I hate — clean toilets, mop floors, clean shower and tubs. That way all I have to do is light housework — vacuuming, laundry, etc. It is a good stress reliever.
2. I stock up when grocery shopping and go less often.
3. Sell or eliminate things causing extra stress and taking up valuable time, sell rental houses, spa, or clutter (have a garage sale).
4. I set up monthly bills to be paid electronically, utility bills, mortgage, phone and cable.
5. I do chores when at my peak energy level (for me mornings).
6.I do things on my way to and from work, such as getting gas and picking up dry cleaning."

Cluster the Jobs by Area

Beth Rosier of Mosford, FL says, "I cluster jobs to be done according to an area. If I am to be a passenger in my car for a period of time I take baby wipes or Windex and paper towels to clean the interior while riding, or some paperwork that can be done, or some professional reading. If I am watching the kids bathe I will do light bathroom cleaning while in there. If I am watching the kids outside I will water the garden, sweep the deck, pull a few weeds, or fertilize the plants. Since I have a large kitchen I can cluster afternoon activities there. While helping with homework I can wash bottles, make formula, prepare meals, and make phone calls. I try to get as much done in a certain area that I have to be in instead of going from here to there."

Cluster Events

"When I entertain, I have several functions in a one to two week period. This saves time cleaning and preparing food. Once the house is clean, I take advantage of it. Also, I serve many of the same dishes and food. Double batches and freezing foods are utilized." Gayle and I agree with Marge on this one, especially the clean house part. We have long joked each other that the two times our house looks its best is when company is expected or it's for sale.

Weekends Free

It's going to get done anyhow. Why let the work pile up until the weekend? Karen Raybould of Chillicothe, OH, has a strategy for freeing her weekends. "I work full time at a radio station. I also own a business that makes and sells old fashioned potato chips. I want my weekends as free as possible to smell the roses."

"<u>Laundry</u> — Twice a week I put a load of laundry in the in the washer before I go to work. I come home for lunch and dry, fold, and put away (as I grab lunch).

<u>Dinners</u> — I always make a little extra so I can freeze it in individual containers. Then, when I'm running late, I can just defrost dinner.

<u>Cleaning</u> — Two nights a week I play tennis. The other three: I vacuum one night; clean bathrooms another; and dust and mop on the third."

Adds Karen, "if I do household chores week nights and during lunch hours, I can truly enjoy two full days on the weekend."

Go with Your Best Time

"Being a night person I prepare my to do list at night before I go to bed," points out Wynne Ellen Vance of Atlanta, GA. "This is a skill I developed as I enlarged my vision when I turned fortyish. I now juggle a full time administrative job, a part time independent beauty consultant business, and a part time volunteer job as a ministry trainer at my church. On top of all this I am enrolled in Bible College on a part time basis."

Suspense List

"I have a tip that helps me remain prioritized and gives me a sense of accomplishment for the tasks completed," writes Ginger Revis of Jacksonville, FL. "It is a new twist on the to do list. I call it a suspense list. I make a standard to do list and assign the tasks a date. I have found this more motivating by assigning dates to my daily tasks. I have found this functions as a quick glance recap of a day timer or monthly planner. Example:

Suspense List
May 1-31
5/1 Pay bills
5/2 Meeting with boss.
5/3 Sally's meeting with teacher
5/4 Get estimate for car
5/6 New sprinklers from Home Depot
5/7 Meet with boss
5/8 Seminar
…and so on…

As I finish each task I cross it off. If I didn't get to the tasks that day I will highlight it. Each morning I review the highlighted items and re-prioritize them. You can also use this as a master plan to create a daily to do list."

Brenda's Basics: a Realistic Approach for an Active Family

Like so many of us, Brenda Mastaler of Williamsburg, VA knows that running a household in today's hyper-active world is a challenge. "We are both working parents who

Ode to Time Management

have a thirty-five minute commute," Brenda writes, "we have two children, ages 10 and 13, who are involved in many extracurricular activities. Both of us parents are heavily involved in volunteer activities in support of the school and athletic club." How to harmonize a hectic household? Here are Brenda's tips:

"1. Delegate! Involve your family.
 2. Have a schedule for chores and follow it religiously.
 3. Use a planning calendar to document individuals' schedules.
 4. Have one meal (dinner) where everyone can regroup, focus, and re-energize from the day's activities.
 5. Rid yourself of unnecessary "shoulds".
 6. Learn to say no.
 7. Everything we do best is simple, basic, and easy.
 8. Sneak away with your spouse several times a year for a personal short retreat.
 9. Organize your house.
10. Map your *off* day.
11. Get kids involved in planning early.
12. Reward yourselves.

"This is a rough outline of how our family of four remains in control of our daily lives and enjoys our experiences. We have realistic approach to managing our time."

Smart Ideas that Work Every Day

Nancy DuCharme of Bourbonnais, IL shares with us a rapid-fire blast of valuable ideas. "Hire help if you can afford it for housekeeping and other tasks. When overwhelmed, get some Post-it Notes. Write one task on each note. As you complete the task, throw the note away. As the jobs dwindle, so will the feeling of being over-whelmed. Divide up the household tasks. Set rewards and consequences if tasks do or do not get done. Have a job jar; everyone in the family picks a job and does it; this can make it fun and promotes family teamwork. Celebrate with a pizza when everything is done. Do the most unwanted tasks first; the weight on your shoulders will seem lighter. Order pizza once a week without guilt. Simplify your life. Do you really need twenty-five pairs of shoes all over the floors? Clean out the house, have a garage sale, give items to charity. Less is best and will de-clutter your mind as well as your house."

Dad's Perspective

David Alfes of Easton, MD, has ideas that resonate well. David suggests:

"1. Make lunches the night before to save time in the morning.

2. Sit down and help with homework (so kids have more time for chores!)

3. Talk at dinner about practices, times to be picked up, when the dance begins.

4. The day before, decide what is for dinner and who is going to cook it.

5. Shave in the evening to save four minutes in the morning to drink a cup of coffee and read the sports page.

6. Every member gets a few hours a week for personal time. Dad plays golf. Mom gets out with the girls. Courtney spends the time on the phone (15 years old). Lauren rents a video."

Shopping List Template

Your computer can help streamline your grocery shopping. "I made a shopping list template on my computer," says LaVon Feeley of Rancho Cucamonga, CA. It is on an 8 ½ x 11 page and I categorize it in three columns: refrigerated; personal, cleaning, other; shelf items. The benefit is I can look at the list and check off what we need. If I need something that's not on the list I later add it to the template. There is a line next to each item for quantity. Example:

_____ hamburger	_____ cream of chicken soup
_____ chicken	_____ salad dressing

"Also, I use one index card that lists every main meal we enjoy. This makes planning easy," LaVon adds.

Ideas That'll Speed Up Your Productivity

Secretary Shirley Toney of Urbana, IL scores a direct hit with her thoughts on doing more in less time at home.

"1. Use a list of things to be done, usually putting first the most difficult, critical, or challenging.

2. Know the time frame and operate accordingly.

3. Work in the most encountered area first, and work your way back to the least encountered. Anything you are unable to get to — hide in closets, stash under beds, stuff in the lowest drawer, or roll behind locked doors.

4. Travel to the farthest place first (if time permits). Hit the other places during the return trip. If purchasing food, do it on the last leg of the trip.

5. Wash clothes at the laundry either early in the morning or late in the evening to avoid crowds."

Plan Ahead to Drop Food Preparation Time to Just Minutes

As a licensed practical nurse, Vanessa Fuksa of Woukomis, OK has her hands full, time-wise. To maximize her off duty hours, Vanessa says on a day off she will "make several meals and freeze them in storage containers. When I come home from a long day's work, I pop one in the microwave, open a can of vegetables, and have a meal in minutes. That leaves more time for family or fun."

Create More Free Time at Home

Carol Herz, a training and development coordinator at the University of California in Los Angeles (UCLA), serves up four cool tips for creating more free time at home.

"1. When I come home from work, I don't sit down until I've done at least three things. Because once I sit down, I often don't get as much done.

2. Make lasagna (it's good for more than one day).

3. Prepare meals in the crockpot. It takes as little as five minutes to put it a crockpot and it smells *great* when you get home.

4. Go ahead — hire someone to clean your house really well once a month. My time is valuable and sometimes the best use of it is in letting go of some of the home responsibilities. It's worth the money and relieves a lot of stress."

Ready to Go

Kathy Ingulsrud, a sales representative in Shoreview, MN offers some tidy suggestions for an active, on-the-go lifestyle. She wrote this about her desk at work, but we think it's great, too, for a desk at home.

"1. I always keep the cul-de-sac neighborhood phone list in my day timer so I can call for baby-sitters, lawn cutters, etc. at work.

2. I keep extra items at my desk like various colored hose, birthday, and thank you cards.

3. My workout bag has to be stocked and ready to go at all times."

Christmas Presents to Yourself

"I shop all year long to buy for thirty plus people at Christmas, says Kimberly Munt of Florida. "Presents are stored in the attic until time to be wrapped. The deadline is December 1st for wrapping as almost 100% of the presents are shipped."

Diane Warner of Big Lake, MN is an early shopper, too. "This has worked for the last ten years! I have all my Christmas shopping finished before Thanksgiving and avoid all the crowds. In fact, most of the time the presents are all wrapped before Thanksgiving. The hassle of the season is out of the way and I can enjoy Christmas, which is a present to myself and my family because I'm not stressed out. Hint: The family does name drawing at Christmas so you have all year to shop."

THE LAST WORD

Many of these tips, tricks, and shortcuts are deceptively simple (like LaVon Feeley's idea of making a grocery shopping template that reflects the tastes and buying habits of *your family* in order to reduce shopping time, ensure buying the right things, and staying focused as a way to save money that might be spent impulsively). And they can have a big impact.

Does this sound like you? Sue Cermak, an associate financial analyst who lives in Fairview, PA, has her act together. "Organization is the key to spending quality time with my family," writes Sue. Her list reads like a recap of the ideas you just read. We offer her ideas to you as a quick review:

Sue's TimeSmart Tips

- "Cook meals during weekends and freeze
- Pack lunches, diaper bag, and lay out the next day's wardrobe the night prior
- Do laundry and clean house when children are sleeping
- Write checks during lunch hour

- Hire a cleaning person to perform certain duties like scrubbing
- Have spouse assist in running errands and grocery shopping
- Write list prior to grocery shopping
- Stock up at grocery to save trips to store
- Take dress shirts to cleaners
- Start your Christmas shopping in September
- Call-in your prescription refills at pharmacy
- Use to do lists
- Don't over-extend yourself
- Screen calls and return calls when you have the time"

Steven Todd of Austin, TX reminds us, "time is like money. Everyday you get twenty-four hours to spend. You can't save it or use it for the next day. It is like a trust fund, but you can't save it — so spend it wisely."

May you live all the days of your life.
JONATHAN SWIFT

Being TimeSmart
Turn Your Thoughts to Tools

I. Identify TimeSmart ideas of your own that are inspired by this chapter.

II. Solution seeking
1. Identify a productivity sapping challenge you occasionally face.

2. If you could change it from challenge to ideal, what would ideal be like?

3. Put check marks next to 3 ideas in this chapter that can help you successfully overcome the challenge.

4. Identify action steps to change the situation for the better and indicate when you will start each one.

INDEX

Thank You

Danny Thomas said if he had known how nearly impossible it was to become a TV star, he never could have done it. Writing two books simultaneously is challenging, too! (The companion to this book is *TimeSmart: How Real People Really Get Things Done at Work*).

Thank you to all who contributed to turn this idea into reality. Extra-special thanks for their extra-special assistance goes to:

Amanda & Jimmy Smart
Frances Ergas
Don & Marilyn Smart
Geri Godfrey
Jeanne Chambers
Debra & Paul Manning
Sudee Campbell
Judith Lamond
Rita VanVracken
Paula Chance
Karin Gaul

and the HUNDREDS of people
who cared enough to write out their personal
how tos *and share them with us so that we could*
share them with the world.

Thank you, Darlene Nicholas, for carefully
designing the look of the books.

Thank you, John McLaughlin, for doing 18
clever illustrations in a very short time.

About John McLaughlin

A multi-talented artist and illustrator, John McLaughlin makes his home in Atlanta, Georgia. His insightful wit and clever drawings touch the funny bone of the child in each of us. John holds a degree in psychology from C.W. Post and attended the Rhode Island School of Design. And he is the father of an 8 year old son (not hard to see where his inspiration comes from!). Watch for his work; you'll be seeing more and more.

To reach John for information on illustrating your promotional material, advertising, reports, or other projects, call (770) 587-9784.

About Gayle & Doug Smart

Gayle is from Long Island, NY. She and Doug met at Universidad de las Americas in Cholula, Mexico, married, and set up house in New Orleans, LA. She is the proud mother of Amanda and Jimmy. She works with Doug in the speaking business.

Doug believes whole-heartedly in the rhythms of success. Growing up in New Orleans, Louisiana, he internalized his father's advice, "if you want to quickly become a success at something, be around people who are already successful at it." Following the beat, Doug started a life-long journey to uncover success secrets. Applying the right principles at the right time earned him a *Lifetime Sales Achievement Award* at age 28! And now, over a decade later, Doug works closely with his clients to share what he's learned so that they, too, enhance the success they were born to achieve by igniting flames that burst from pilot lights to bon fires; the result: increased personal satisfaction and increased productivity that leads directly to increased bottom line profitability!

A nationally recognized speaker, consultant, and author, with 900 presentations (to date), Doug is acclaimed for his energetic and straight-forward, fun and sincere approach to discovering workable solutions for immediate return.

He has done repeat engagements for groups as diverse as AT&T, Rockwell International, VA Medical Centers, Hospitality Sales & Marketing Association, University of Illinois, and NASA.

As founder and president of Doug Smart Seminars in Atlanta, Georgia, Doug is still collecting ideas and secrets of successful people for his audiences, all of which are experiencing dramatic change in today's hotly competitive marketplace. Membership in National Speakers Association, Georgia Speakers Association and Meeting Professionals International, plus in-depth interviews, keeps Doug current on rapidly changing trends.

Doug has developed a series of presentations and seminars focused on the importance of developing and maintaining personal resiliency and strength to help you fulfill your personal and professional potential so that no matter where you are or what you are doing, the next twelve months can be your best year yet! This ***SMART IDEAS***™ series is packed with practical information on success in handling change, developing personal support networks, personal development, and time management. Doug's observation: *top achievers constantly fine-tune the rhythms of success they hear deep inside!*

To reach Doug for information about speaking for your convention or organization, please call your Speakers Bureau.

Need Additional Copies?

Copy and Complete this form and send to:

Fax Orders to: 770-587-1050
Phone Orders to: 770-587-9784
Or Mail Orders to: James & Brookfield Publishers
                            P.O. Box 768024
                            Roswell, GA 30076

Send to:

_____

Name

_____

Address   MS/Apt. #

_____

City State   Zip
(   ) _____

Telephone Number

Please fill my order for the following:

TimeSmart:
How Real People Really Get Things Done at <u>Work</u>   _____ copies

TimeSmart:
How Real People Really Get Things Done at <u>Home</u>   _____ copies

Price List:

$17.00 for each book x _____ copies = $_____

Georgia residents add 7% sales tax $_____

**Add $3.00 for first book and $.75 per additional
book for shipping and handling** $_____
**Amount Enclosed (*check or money order*)
or Charge my credit Card** $_____

(Check appropriate Card)   ☐Visa   ☐MasterCard

_____

Account Number   Expiration Date

_____

Signature if ordering by Credit Card (required)
Thank You for Your Order!